Rebuilding Your House of Self-Respect

Men recovering in group from childhood sexual abuse

By Tom Wilken

Library and Archives Canada Cataloguing in Publication

Wilken, Tom
Rebuilding Your House of Self-Respect: Men recovering in group
from childhood sexual abuse

ISBN 978-0-9809991-0-5

1. Male sexual abuse victims—rehabilitation. 2. Adult child sexual
abuse victims—rehabilitation. 3. Male sexual abuse victims—
counselling of. 4. Adult child sexual abuse victims—counselling
of. 5. Group psychotherapy. 6. Child sexual abuse—treatment. 7.
Self-esteem in men.

HV6570.W54 2008   616.85'836906   C2008-903008-7

© 2008 Tom Wilken

ISBN 978-0-9809991-0-5

Publisher
Hope and Healing Associates
Box 53, Erieau, Ontario N0P 1N0
silencetohope@hotmail.com

Editing and Project Management
Debbie Elicksen, Freelance Communications,
Calgary, Alberta

Design and Production
Bobbie-Jo Bergner, Mind's Design Studio, Calgary, Alberta

Printing
Transcontinental, Sherbrooke, Quebec

Rebuilding Your House of Self-Respect: Men recovering in group
from childhood sexual abuse – Second Edition
Printed and Bound in Canada
Copyright 2008

Dedication

This book is dedicated to the circle of seven male survivors who contributed their comments throughout this book. May their courage and strength be an inspiration to us all.

To all survivors of sexual abuse — there is hope.

Acknowledgements

When considering whom to acknowledge, I am reluctant to single out any one person or agency. There are so many people who made this book possible, both by participating directly or indirectly. All these good folks played an important role, and their contributions are most welcomed.

I am grateful to my loving partner Doris. She has been by my side throughout the entire process. Our children are truly a gift for us, and we couldn't be prouder of Jamie, Brent and Pat Wilken, and Melissa, Gordie, and Spencer King. Five of the children have grown and found their own nest, but we are still fortunate enough to have Spencer living with us. This may be my last opportunity to say I can still take Spencer in a game of one on one basketball, so I must embrace the moment.

Family support is always welcome when working on sensitive topics. My brother Rick Wilken and my cousin Jackie Brown are the first people who come to mind. Thanks to my Aunt Mary Neelands for reminding me how proud my mother, Margaret Wilken, would be, knowing that her son has a passion to help people in pain.

The second edition of this book is made possible by the generosity of Hope and Healing Associates, the Canadian Centre for Abuse Awareness, and the Diocese of London.

I am incredibly thankful to Daniel Cahill and Bob McGuire. They are not only my friends, but were instrumental in sending free copies of the first edition throughout the

Country of Canada. Ellen Campbell and Lynne MacDonell have always been supportive with any endeavors that helps promote men in their healing process.

Dr. Fred Mathews is the man responsible for writing the foreword for this book. His advocacy for victims of abuse is admirable. I hope his wish for including male sexual abuse survivors into the circle of compassion happens in my lifetime.

My faith in Debbie Elicksen from Freelance Communications has proven to be a wise decision. Her skills and guidance have been a breath of fresh air. Thanks to Bobbie-Jo Bergner of Mind's Design Studio for her ability to make the vision become reality.

Table of Contents

Foreword

Jonathan Swift once said that you cannot reason someone out of a belief if they were never reasoned into it. Indeed, beliefs based on habit, bias, or ignorance can be the most resistant to change. But what if those beliefs were bringing great suffering and harm to half the population of a country? What if those beliefs were being perpetuated by the public, helping professionals and people in positions of authority and power? Would they be changed? Could they be changed? Possibly, but first they would have to be acknowledged, and that acknowledgment would require great humility and generosity of spirit.

The beliefs of which I am speaking have to do with the lives of men, particularly adult males who are survivors of child sexual abuse. And the men I am talking about are not faceless strangers; they are our fathers, brothers, cousins, husbands, grandfathers, uncles, the boy next door, our classmates, our work colleagues, the man next to us on the bus, and the males we pass on the sidewalk everyday. What are some of these beliefs? "'Real men' can or should take care of themselves." "Men don't suffer lasting harm from violence, abuse, or aggression." "Men who were abused as children should 'just snap out of it.'" "Being harsh and abusive toward boys toughens them up and makes men out of them."

These beliefs are not just harmful to male survivors — they are dangerous to all male children. They are dangerous because they perpetuate the idea that the use of force, aggression, and abuse are acceptable means of socializing boys. They excuse harsh and abusive child rearing practices toward male children. They support the sexual exploitation of boys. They silence male victims and suppress their stories. They cast a shadow across our claims of being an inclusive, compassionate and egalitarian society.

I have been advocating for male victims for about two decades. When I first started speaking publicly about the need to develop support services for male survivors, I used to get challenged about the "low numbers" of male victims in academic studies of child abuse. At first I was puzzled how anyone could equate supposed "low numbers" with "no need for services." I still wonder what number would satisfy these people and evoke their compassion.

Thankfully, the literature on male survivors has expanded over the years. We now know much more about the widespread prevalence of sexual violence toward boys and young men. We also know that academic studies of child abuse provide only a part of the story. Many adult male survivors continue to "hide" in the statistics on, for example, suicide, alcoholism, addictions, mental illness, workaholism, and premature death. Unfortunately, despite this growth in knowledge about male survivors, services are still few in number.

Male survivors often avoid conventional counselling services because they do not feel welcome. Also, we have shamed males for so long in order to socialize them to be self-sacrificing, that we have cultured out of many men any feeling of deserving compassion and support. Those courageous souls who do take the risk and reach out often don't return because therapists are not trained to work with male specific issues or their techniques are based on the experiences of female survivors.

The time has come for us to mature as a society and to expand the Canadian conversation on interpersonal violence and aggression. We need more funding allocated for research, program development, and the training of helpers to support male survivors. We need to make common the stories of male survivors' trials and experiences. We need to light out the shadows of ignorance about men abused as children and apply reason to our collective project to achieve healing as a society.

Tom Wilken has provided the helping community with an important and vital resource to help facilitate a healing journey for men recovering from childhood sexual abuse. But he has also done something very brave. He listened to hurting adult male survivors, believed them, wrote down their stories, and decided to share that information with others who refuse to exclude men from the circle of compassion. He is a quiet, gentle hero whose generosity of spirit is evident on every page of this informed and inspiring guide. He, and those who walk with him, are breaking important ground in the struggle for true social justice and cultural transformation.

Dr. Fred Mathews
Toronto, Canada
March 2003

Introduction

Welcome to the second edition of *Rebuilding Your House of Self-Respect: Men in group recovering from childhood sexual abuse*. There have been a lot of changes that have taken place since the first edition. The first part of this book will provide you with some facts and figures about male sexual abuse, followed by seven survivors telling their stories. Five years after these brave men completed their support group experience, they provided a more in depth overview of their healing process.

Part two has been dedicated to the ten stages of recovery. These chapters will bring you on a journey through the entire healing process. Anyone unable to attend a support group can feel free to answer the questions asked in this section. This will offer you an opportunity to follow an extensive process that covers an entire group experience.

The last section, part three, provides information for partners, families, and friends. It also speaks to caregivers, such as members of a support team and counsellors. Several exercises are given to provide further education and awareness.

Thousands of copies of the first edition were distributed throughout the province of Ontario and across Canada through the We Want to Know Project and the Silence to Hope Project, in partnership with the Canadian Centre for Abuse Awareness and the Diocese of London Ontario. A large portion of this second edition will be used for a similar purpose. We want to enhance our education and awareness programs in hopes of creating a safer and supportive environment for male victims of sexual abuse.

A recap on the first edition

Sexual abuse is still considered a taboo subject in our society, particularly regarding male victims. Most people are uncomfortable talking about sex, but sexual abuse of boys and men further discomforts because it challenges our stereotypes about men. Various programs stress the needs of women and children. They educate the public and social service agencies about appropriate services but fail to recognize that boy victims rarely deal with their issues until they become adults. We expect men to be strong, self-reliant, and not show any weakness. Adult male survivors of childhood sexual abuse cite such cultural beliefs for their reluctance about revealing their past experiences.

Sexual abuse of males is widespread, underreported and, most importantly, we do not take seriously the need for effective recovery programs. Many people minimize male sexual abuse and reject the large number of recent publicized male abuse cases. Like abuse victims who have not started the journey to recovery, society seems to be stuck in a collective denial. People do not want to believe these terrible things are happening, even though they are occurring in our own communities and covered up by trusted authority figures. Instead of accepting the need for recovery and acting on the problem, people find it easier to deny and minimize the reality of male sexual abuse. Unfortunately, this only discourages male victims from seeking help, protects abusers, and effects longer lasting suffering on victims and their families.

This book does not only represent the voice of a facilitator but also the collective voices of people seeking to help male victims. Male victims of sexual assault have not had a collective voice. This book cannot speak for all victims; however, the voices of numerous male survivors will attempt to speak to you through the following material. They need us to hear these voices and listen to their concerns. Hopefully the insights gained through this project will encourage agencies to provide effective services for men, providing a safety net for men to seek help.

For victims, therapists, and loved ones

This material can help all victims to become empowered and give them an opportunity to regain their physical, mental, and social health. All men can recover from childhood sexual abuse, and this book will provide them with working tools to meet this challenge. By using the information provided, survivors will become more proactive in nurturing relationships with themselves and others.

Counsellors and therapists have been finding this information useful to expand their skills and knowledge in providing services for male victims. Selected service agencies have field-tested this book as a working guide for their own support groups.

Families and support persons will find this book useful to help them understand what their loved ones are experiencing, and to give them a concrete understanding of their role in the recovery process.

The book process

A group of seven men and their facilitator started this book-writing project over a decade ago. Early in the support group journey, it became clear that there was very little written material on male sexual abuse recovery. When members from a male sexual abuse survivor support group expressed an eagerness to help others, the book process began and continued over the next thirteen years.

The group members felt empowered knowing that expressing their pain would help others beyond the group setting. Each group met once a week for two hours over a ten-week time frame. Their comments were recorded, sorted, and categorized into specific areas of conversation. These areas of conversation were then sorted again into potential chapters for this text.

The majority of comments came from three separate groups, lasting over thirty weeks. Six other groups provided their input after the initial comments were documented.

Various people from all walks of life have contributed to this project. Not all of them can be named, however. They include: both male and female survivors, male and female friends and families of survivors, doctors, PhDs, counsellors, social workers, psychotherapists, colleagues, educators, group facilitators, business people, teachers, factory workers, executive directors, publishers, editors, real estate brokers, and members of various support groups.

Facilitators have used the first edition as a model for training other facilitators and as an educational tool for their support group participants. Many people have contributed their time and effort to ensure you, the reader, have reliable, accurate information.

Seven courageous men from group

The original seven men that participated in these groups deserve credit for their extraordinary courage and knowledge. When the opportunity to become part of a group presented itself, the members felt it was long overdue. This was the first time a group of this nature took place in their community. Each of them expressed angry feelings towards their communities for not providing help sooner. They all had concerns regarding the lack of services and educational opportunities for other male survivors. Group members had a strong desire to help others, and three separate groups thought they could get this project started by sharing their comments with you throughout this book.

These men came from various walks of life, each with their own unique experiences. Their abusers also came from various walks of life, such as: police officers, neighbours, babysitters, older friends, family members, and representatives from their church. Older males sexually abused all seven men as children. Three of these men were also sexually abused by women. Several of these men were subjected to multiple abusers, and all them were sexually abused more than once. Most of the men were abused for two or more years. Their perpetrators were known to all of them. Each of their abusers held a position of trust. In every situation, there was an imbalance of power and control, as might be expected with childhood sexual abuse, and every member of the group had a clear recollection of their sexually abusive experience.

Four group participants were employed and the other three were not working at the time the group sessions took place. All of these men have received individual counselling and became knowledgeable on sexual abuse recovery issues. It would be safe to say that each of them was at a different stage of recovery when this material was written. Each participant was sexually abused as a child fifteen to forty years prior to his or her involvement in group. Group participants ranged in ages from twenty-six to fifty-two.

Two of the group participants contacted the police and had their abusers charged. Both felt re-traumatized by the justice system. They wondered why sexual abuse victims are treated like the guilty party. Both court cases took several years to complete.

Seeking help is a sign of strength

Men in general are known for being reluctant to seek health services. Men often deny their vulnerabilities and feel they must portray the illusion of strength. One of the reasons men lack services is because sexual abuse recovery lacks a masculine voice.

It is important to challenge the attitudes and cultural norms of a society that minimizes the existence of male sexual abuse. This material is unique, and to my knowledge, it is the only book that includes the stages of recovery for male sexual abuse survivors.

Let's hope that eventually all victims of sexual abuse will be given equal access to services regardless of race, social status, or gender. This book will help increase the accessibility of information about male sexual abuse recovery and encourage men to reach out for help. If more men disclose the sexual abuse they were subjected to as children, then more support services will be created. As more services are created, more educational information will become available.

About your feelings
when reading this book

Reading books of this nature can be very powerful, and you may experience a wide range of feelings and emotions. That is perfectly normal and natural considering the sensitivity connected to this topic. There may be times when you may need to put this book aside, and there is nothing wrong with that. Travel at a pace you are comfortable with, however, growth often comes from being comfortably uncomfortable.

Be sceptical about what you read, and form your own opinions based on what you believe is right for you. Select the information that is most useful for you, and put aside the rest. This information can be like a planted seed, which may not flourish until a later date.

You may be surprised by the insight and knowledge of some group participants. All participants had received extensive individual counselling prior to their group experience. Some of these men are avid readers and are knowledgeable on recovery issues. The quotes in this book were selected from well over a thousand comments. It may seem that questions were simply asked and replied to in one session. In reality, each set of quotes may represent a collection of responses that were documented over the thirty-week time frame. The quotes in this text do not follow a natural progression from session number one of the first group, to session number ten of that same group. Questions and responses may have come from various sessions throughout several groups.

Voice, language, and male culture

I will be using the terms "victim" and "survivor" throughout this text, but I also recognize the limitations of these words. These terms are commonly used in abuse related material but can discount the aspects of a person's life that are both healthy and productive. Some men prefer the term *thriver*. They view themselves as not only surviving, but also living and thriving. Sexual abuse is something that happens to people; it is not who they are. As men evolve in their recovery processes, they are less likely to see themselves as a "victim" or "survivor." These limited terms will be used until something better comes along.

Men need to develop and use their own language in recovery. Unfortunately, much of the existing language of therapy and recovery is distinctly feminine in tone and character. Healthy male culture includes: teamwork, equality, brotherhood, and being of service to others. Wounds from sexual abuse can be healed; men can move on.

The focus of this book is the core issues male survivors deal with in support groups and how they work through these issues to enhance their quality of life.

This material is not written as an academic research paper. There are no footnotes, and it is not filled with endless statistics. It is written in plain English, which will hopefully appeal to most readers.

The men who generously contributed their comments were given pseudonyms to protect their privacy.

The journey begins.

Part 1

Male Sexual Abuse: Facts, Impacts, and Effects

Recovering from sexual abuse is a very multi-dimensional topic; however, we live in a society that likes to define mental health issues in one-dimensional terms. Healing from sexual abuse can be a complex problem that requires assistance from others.

This chapter will focus on several aspects of healing. It starts with defining sexual abuse and looks at the number of men who are victimized. How often are men sexually abused, and what are the factors that influence the impact? Group members talk about being annoyed with the mainstream approach to recovery and are confused with how to view themselves. Many issues that survivors encounter are similar to struggles we all face. However, the intensity may differ. Members are looking at methods to take responsibility for their lives and to develop ways to reach inside of themselves for the answers.

What is sexual abuse?

There is no single, universally accepted definition of sexual abuse. In this text, sexual abuse refers to any act of a sexual nature, imposed by one person upon another where there is an imbalance of power and control. The balance of power may be unequal due to: age, economic reasons, social class, physical strength, or psychological

of their lives; however, as the counselling process evolves they identify sexual abuse as their main source of discomfort. Very often, an unresolved sexual abuse history is the engine driving these problems, and men can solve these "primary presenting problems" themselves once they recover in-group. Many men are reluctant to "present" to mental health or abuse services. The approach and exercises in this book, with few exceptions, can be used effectively in men's groups, with trust and in a male voice, without assumptions that the men are mentally ill.

Men from group have a favourite saying: "You cannot change others; you can only change yourself." They may be bitter and angry about the past but recognize that their future belongs to them. Everything they do in life from now on is their choice, and they do have options. Anything they have learned in the past can be unlearned, and they can choose new ways of working towards becoming the person they want to be. Men from RYHSR groups say they are responsible for their feelings and emotions, and others are responsible for theirs. Taking ownership of their individual actions is an empowering RYHSR technique. I emphasize that this is a lengthy process, and we could find no shortcut. It is natural to feel bad before feeling good, but ownership of feelings and proactive group support can reduce the bad times.

We often talk in RYHSR group about a formula Jack Canfield mentioned in one of his self-esteem tapes. Canfield says: E + R = O. That is, **E**vents in our lives, plus our **R**esponses equals the **O**utcome. One definition of insanity includes responding to events in the same way and expecting a different outcome. Male sexual abuse recovery is all about changing the R's, and these men are learning to respond differently to Events so that they can have a more desirable Outcome. This change is not easy. It takes hard work. It takes a lot of soul searching. We must look inwards to change our Responses.

Group members said they spent their lives searching outside of themselves for answers to their problems. They were looking for that one person or one thing that could heal them, often searching from the outside-in. RYHSR group is about learning to change and approach life from the inside out. They were amazed that the answers to their questions were within them all along. Their own greatest resource was, and is, themselves. Nobody can do their work for them. Others may assist them on their journeys, but the journey is theirs. Nobody can grieve their losses or feel for them. The RYHSR group provided support and information, but these men did the work. To these journeymen goes the credit.

Survivors and Their Stories

Men from group share their stories with the intent to provide you with an overview of their healing process. They were interviewed again five years after they completed the group process. This period of time gave them an opportunity to process the healing journey and provide an accurate overview. Their sincere hope is that other people in pain will benefit from their openness and honesty about a very sensitive and vulnerable topic.

Each of these men will provide you with an overview of their abusive experience, how they were affected, and what happened when they attempted to reach out for help. They will explain their views on their group experience and give practical advice for other survivors.

Jim's Story

Jim is a forty-year-old man who was married for fifteen years to his second wife. He expresses a deep love for her and their two children. His first marriage began at the age of nineteen and ended when he was twenty-four.

The abuse

Jim looks at his childhood with both appreciation and regret. He expressed love for his parents but was concerned about a lack of communication with various members in the family. As an adult, he struggled with expressing himself to family members, who coped by avoiding conversations that included emotion.

When Jim was eleven, a local minister in his forties showed an interest in befriending him, and he joyfully accepted this opportunity. He was delighted that someone was offering love, affection, and spiritual guidance. This "man of the cloth" was just what he wanted to enrich his life.

As time evolved, he became confused about his relationship with this man, who was well respected in the community. He was baffled one day when the minister attempted to kiss him. Even though Jim was concerned, he was still very interested in their friendship. As time evolved, the minister made repeated sexual advances that included fondling and fellatio. He questioned why this minister would want to perform fellatio on a boy to the point of ejaculation, and why a little boy would have to stop a religious leader from putting a finger into his rectum. When he confronted the minister with these concerns, he was reassured that in "God's eyes," it was okay for him to do these things.

One of his most haunting memories goes back to a situation in the minister's private office. The abuser had taken Jim's clothes off and was performing fellatio on him when someone knocked on the closed door. The person on the other side of the door asked if everything was okay. Jim froze in total shock, unable to speak, even though part of him wanted to scream. The minister immediately assured the enquirer that everything was fine and that person went about their business. Thirty years later, Jim still feels guilty for not speaking up. He thought the abuse was his fault because he did not cry out for help when given the opportunity.

He talks about having mixed emotions when he contemplated telling his father. On one hand, he was scared, thinking he would not be believed. On the other hand, he was frightened what his dad might do to the minister. He wanted to protect the minister and, at the same time, find some way to sort through his confusion. He felt the only way to keep the peace was continued silence. Jim also mentioned being confused with not understanding that the situation was abusive. He stated, "If you can't trust a minister, who can you trust?" As the minister continued to abuse him, he continued to feel confused and thought he was caught up in a homosexual act. Jim was repeatedly sexually abused by this man for six years.

The effects

Jim still feels shame when he thinks about how his body responded to these inappropriate sexual acts. Wondering why something that was so abusive could also feel so good at times. He remembers a sense of satisfaction when the minister would praise him in front of family and others. Jim not only felt betrayed by this spiritual role model but by his own body.

As an adult, he tried to keep the "ghosts" of the past away, but it became a full- time chore. He went through periods of not eating for days, followed by excessive eating that he described as gorging himself. When this could not keep the ghost from the past away, he turned to other addictions, which included smoking marijuana, consuming alcohol, gambling, and sex.

Jim looks back at a lifetime of feeling disoriented. Severe headaches seemed like a normal part of living. He was experiencing over one hundred and fifty migraines a year. At one time, his anxiety levels escalated to the point he was hospitalized for depression, combined with suicidal thoughts.

He clearly remembers how helpless he felt during this hospital stay and feeling miserable when listening to the psychiatrist, who was recommending medications. Jim knew exactly what was causing his discomfort. All he could think about was the family minister and his childhood. Jim was experiencing the same sensations he had when he was younger and heard a knock on the door at the minister's private office. At that time, he could not tell the person on the other side of the door what was happening. This time, he was unable to tell the psychiatrist what was wrong. Again, he became numb and could not speak. Jim says it felt like there was a child inside of him that wanted to scream "help me!" The hospital stay ended, and Jim went home with several prescribed medications. He looks back now with amazement, surprised at how strong the urge to keep silent can be. Jim was getting prescriptions for all kinds of pills that he knew would not make the problem go away. Even though his loving wife talked about ending their marriage, he remained silent and could not bring himself to talk about the past.

Jim talks very openly about his past struggles with his sexuality. As a child and throughout early adulthood, he was confused about homosexuality. Thinking he had taken part in a homosexual relationship, he was sure he must be gay. His sexual experimentation with other men was a source of embarrassment for him. As time evolved, he realized he was heterosexual. When he came to the understanding that he preferred sexual relationships with women, he was very angry with the minister who abused him under the guise of spiritual role modelling.

Excessive masturbation was of great concern for Jim. He said he would think of young boys while he masturbated and would imagine doing the same kind of acts to them as had happened to him. Jim thought masturbation would help erase the troubling thoughts he was having. He felt that by ejaculating through masturbation he would not turn his thoughts into action. The frequency of masturbation also caused concerns in his relationship. He talks about feeling shame for this activity and not having any sexual energy left for his partner.

Reaching out and rebuilding

Jim kept silent for one year after being sexually assaulted by the family minister, over a six-year time frame. His brother-in-law was a minister, and he thought this would be a good place to break silence. At first, his sister's husband was very angry towards the other minister and supportive towards Jim. After various discussions about God and sexuality, Jim was told it was okay with God for people of the same gender to have sexual relations, but only if they cared for each other. The idea was acceptable for the moment, but what transpired next was confusing. For the next year, Jim was frequently masturbated by his sister's husband without her knowledge. One day, she told Jim to stop coming by the house because she felt he had too many problems.

Jim retreated back to silence and struggled alone until he was married. He was unsure about his decision but reached out and explained to his first wife the circumstances in his past. He explained the past sexual abuse and how he responded or coped with being victimized. At first, there was a sense of relief, but then she started using things he told her against him. As time passed, he regretted breaking silence. He became uncomfortable with himself and his wife. They no longer enjoyed intimate moments with each other and a divorce followed. This reinforced his belief that keeping silent may be the best course of action.

Jim's second marriage challenged his decision to remain silent, and he eventually told his new wife. They were having marital problems, and it was starting to take its toll on both of them. She thought it was unusual that he would not interact with the children in any way that involved touch. He refused to change them or hug them. Jim mentions being scared to touch his children for fear of recreating the fantasies he had while masturbating. His relationship with his wife was deteriorating and she encouraged him to seek help.

The first day of counselling was described as a big scary step. During the first session, he remembers an inner voice officer exposed himself, and Pete was coerced to giving him fellatio. Pete's pants were ripped off, and the officer forced him into anal intercourse. When the police officer was finished, he threw Pete out of the automobile. Once Pete regained his strength, he put his clothes back on and walked home.

Pete's thoughts evolved around past comments made by the policeman. He was told to keep his mouth shut, and if he talked, it would be easy to make him disappear. The officer told him he would be taken to a big city and sold for one hundred dollars. Pete did not take this threat lightly, and he believed this threat was real. Fortunately for Pete, the officer was transferred to a new area, and the physical nature of the abuse ended that day. This officer, who was a menace to society, was passed on to the next unsuspecting community.

The effects

In elementary school, Pete excelled academically. After the victimization ended, he attempted to put the abuse behind him. He explained that effects of the abuse are like having your insides turned into a knot, and you freeze up. It's like your mind separates itself from your body. From that moment on, he felt like damaged goods.

As a teenager, he masked his feelings with food to the point of obesity. Several years later, food no longer kept the memories at rest, and he became addicted to methamphetamines. Staying high seemed easier than openly expressing the unpleasantness of the past.

One day, on his way to class at university, he had a significant flashback, which resulted in a suicide attempt, combined with a continual escalation of other concerns. He survived the suicide attempt only because the electrical cord secured around his neck broke free from its anchor. Heightened levels of anxiety and difficulty concentrating on his studies resulted in his dropping out of school.

Pete talked about extreme low self-esteem and how he would isolate himself from others. He was uncomfortable being around people and preferred spending time alone. Pete described himself as worthless and refused to take credit for any of his accomplishments. Struggling to interact with others was a challenge. He would become easily jealous of others and did not trust them. Pete spent most of his life avoiding any possible situation that could trigger upsetting thoughts or memories connected to the past.

Fear was not an easy emotion to manage. Any sight of a police car would put him into an immediate internal frenzy. What seemed like little things or ideas would cause him to panic, creating intense anxiety. Keeping steady employment became impossible. Escalating concerns resulted in Pete being admitted into a psychiatric hospital.

Reaching out and rebuilding

Pete told his father the same night after being forced into sexual acts at gunpoint. Pete remembers how frightened he was when telling his dad about rectal bleeding due to the anal intercourse. His father's response was not exactly what he wanted to hear, as he was told to forget about it.

was thrilled with these tickets and went back to visit the man one more time. After being escorted to the back of a tent, this man put his arms around Bill and attempted to kiss him. This one-time occurrence bothered Bill, and his confusion about sexuality escalated.

When Bill was a young boy, he remembers his older brother displaying some strange behaviour with his other siblings. The oldest brother would take others to secluded areas of the house and engage in secretive acts. Bill was never fond of his oldest sibling, but one day a lot of positive attention started coming his way. His brother was six years older, and until that day, Bill felt unimportant to him. He told Bill he would teach him what big kids do and proceeded to fondle him. Over the next two years, the fondling escalated to oral sex and eventually forced anal intercourse. Bill commented that his brother did all kinds of crazy things to him but one of his most confusing memories included having to watch this older sibling masturbate to the point of ejaculation. He refers to this experience as an unwanted education for a young innocent boy who was incapable of understanding.

Bill was an altar boy at the local church at the time his oldest brother was victimizing him. He became concerned and asked his brother if what he was doing was spiritually wrong. Bill was told that God likes them to do these things but does not want them to talk about it with anyone. Bill bought into his brother's stories, even though he remembers feeling somewhat suspicious.

Eventually his father found out that his oldest son was manipulating the other children in the family into performing sexual acts. Bill remembers the discussion that followed between his father, his brother, and himself, as if it happened yesterday. His father briefly explained the situation in the context of an inappropriate homosexual act. Bill was completely numb and could not say a word. He was left with intense shame and sensed the abuse was his fault. Bill wondered why he wasn't asked if he was okay or how he felt about the whole situation. The result of his father's intervention was an understanding that this situation would not be talked about again.

While the abuse was taking place, Bill was not aware it was abusive. As time passed, he became concerned about the imbalance of power between his brother and himself. Bill had threatened to tell his father prior to their dad finding out about the abuse. His brother told him that nobody would believe him, and if he talked, he would be in big trouble. Bill kept silent for the next twenty-five years.

The effects

Bill recalls never feeling as good as the next guy. He had fears that if other people got to know the "real" him, they would recognize he was sexually abused as a child. Bill said he created a "false-self" as a way of showing others that he was not hurting inside. He often expressed himself in a fashion that was opposite to how he really felt. When he felt lonely and vulnerable, he portrayed an image of being strong and in control.

Feelings of low self worth were evident throughout his life. Bill talks about feeling dirty and thinking it was "his entire fault." He was confused, not knowing what, or who, to believe in. He described the sexual abuse as if he was sold "a bad bill of goods" by someone he trusted, and he bought into it, hook, line, and sinker. The cost of this losing trust in others was enormous. He wondered if anyone was trustworthy. In the future, how could he know if someone was befriending him only to betray him? He questioned that if you can't trust family, who can you trust?

Bill said the abuse was always in the back of his mind and how he thought he was good at keeping buried these deep, dark secrets from the past. He masked his feelings with alcohol and drug use, but as time passed and other issues started to build up, this skill became less effective.

Healthy sexuality was a struggle until his early forties. The uncertainties around love and sex, combined with childhood experiences, left him in a long term state of confusion. Bill talked about not knowing the true meaning of intimacy and how he developed a self-defeating pattern of poor choices that included unhealthy masturbation and visiting prostitutes. Even though he felt these behaviours were wrong, he felt out of control. The shame connected to these actions created anxiety and depression to the point where medication was needed to fight the blue moods he was experiencing.

Reaching out and rebuilding

As mentioned earlier, the first person to become aware of the sexual abuse in the family was his father. Even though his other siblings were sexually abused, they never talked about each other's experiences, and some still refuse to acknowledge that part of their past. Bill felt his father's way of handling the situation encouraged silence and not healing. Bill is often more bitter towards his dad than his older brother. He hates the weakness he sees in his father. He wonders why he was not there for him as a child and why he still refuses to talk about the situation as an adult.

Twenty years after the abuse took place, Bill was facing the possibility of a divorce from his wife. Dealing with the stress of the relationship and the memories of the past became too exhausting. He said an emotional overload resulted in a full-blown depression. Feeling like he had to tell someone, he was jolted into talking to his wife. Bill mentions breaking silence was the hardest thing he had ever done, even though it felt like a big weight was lifted off his shoulders. His wife was supportive in the beginning and encouraged him to seek counselling.

The marriage stayed intact for the next five years, and Bill continued working on himself. He became confused when something unexpected happened. The healthier he became, the more unhappy his wife was. He thinks his honesty about the ripple effects of the sexual abuse contributed to the eventual ending of his marriage. Bill also talked about other unhealthy dynamics in their relationship and how he could not do the work for both of them.

Going for counselling was not an easy task. Bill remembers wanting help so desperately but was terrified to talk to another person, and especially to a man. So many questions ran through his mind. After several years of individual counselling, Bill took advantage of the opportunity to join a support group.

Five years later

How were support groups helpful?

- "I knew I was not alone."
- "I could be myself."
- "People accepted me and validated my feelings connected to the past."
- "They helped me to explore options I never thought of."

Bill felt support groups gave him an opportunity to step away from silence and be accepted by others who were struggling with similar situations in life. He talks about sadness that others in society are not as understanding as fellow group members.

Are you in a better place now? How are you different compared to when you first reached out for help?

- "I am a much better person now."
- "Working from the inside-out compared to the outside-in has given me the opportunity to love and accept myself just the way I am."
- "Connecting with others and being intimate (not sexual) with both genders allows me to feel connected to others."
- "My empathy for others' pain is more realistic now."
- "I love myself just the way I am."
- "I have a better relationship with God, and I'm in a much better place spiritually."

- "I know it was not my fault, and I no longer take the blame for the perpetrators actions."
- "I have learned to forgive myself and others."

When Bill started recovery, he talked about: having no contact with his immediate family, confusion with spirituality, not feeling as good as the next guy, his abusive experience always being in the back of his mind, struggles with his sexuality.

Bill now has regular contact with his family, except for the older brother who sexually abused him. Bill says he feels good that he has forgiven him but does not wish to be part of his life.

He has reconnected with his past religion and feels more comfortable about his relationship with God. His struggles have brought him to a much better spiritual place. Although recovery seemed too hard at times, he feels it has made him a better person.

He is still happily employed and does not struggle as much with feelings of inferiority. Bill seemed amazed that the topic of sexual abuse was so consuming for years, and how he rarely thinks about that part of his past. It is simply something that happened to him and not part of his core identity.

Past sexuality concerns still brings up feelings of guilt, but he feels good that he no longer struggles with sexual confusion. He has been in a loving relationship for the past three years and enjoys intimacy more than he ever has in his whole life.

Steve began taking money from the wallet each day. That was his way of punishing the teacher for not listening. He thought sooner or later, the teacher would notice the money missing and give Steve the attention he wanted. Once the teacher became aware of what was taking place, the police were called and an investigation followed. Steve was convicted and sent to reform school for fifteen months. He is still bitter and wonders why the teacher did not try to help him find someone he could talk to.

The morning after being sexually abused in jail, Steve confronted a guard and reported being raped and forced into anal intercourse. The guard said he hoped Steve had learned a lesson and would not be returning to jail again. To this day, Steve notices he has a lack of respect for any authority figure. The teacher's and the guard's responses reinforced a belief that he was not important enough to be helped. Since nobody cared about him, he stopped caring about himself.

Three decades later and after many years of drug abuse, he decided to seek help by approaching several agencies. He was eventually referred to the Sexual Assault Crisis Centre. Even though he was still hesitant and thought nobody cared, he went to his appointments anyway. He became aware that even though he had been alone as a child, he did not have to struggle by himself as an adult. He recalls that as a nice feeling.

When the opportunity to join a group became available, Steve energetically decided to become a member. He feels that RYHSR group is the single most therapeutic experience that any survivor could have.

Five years later

How were support groups helpful?

- "If it were not for individual counselling and group, I would be dead."
- "It gave me another chance at life."
- "Nobody in society believed me, but people here do."
- "One thing I learned from coming for counselling was that I am not the problem."
- "We can come and cry and help each other."
- "It felt nice that others cared; finally someone cared."
- "I removed the blame from myself; I always believed it was me."
- "Everyday I leave group, I feel overwhelmed. A lot of pressure is off me, like a chip or weight removed from shoulders. It feels like I am chipping away at a dark fungus that had been built up inside of me."

Steve felt that the support group was the single most important part of his recovery process. He wishes groups had been available to him sooner, but was thankful to be part of something that made such a positive impact on his life.

Are you in a better place now? How are you different compared to when you first reached out for help?

- "I can work through my problems now without the need for medications and anger. Even though I still struggle with sex, I enjoy intimacy with my partner."

- "I am much closer with my wife now. I was able to tell her about what I was going through and share my story with her. She understands me now.

- "I am more involved in my community."

- "I do not rush around like a mad man; I take my time; I do what I have to do and enjoy my life."

- "I still get depressed at times, but I always seem to work through it."

- "I do not want to go out and punch and fight now."

Steve talked about several concerns including: his desire to stay in jail as a way of avoiding interactions with people, lack of community involvement, alcohol and drug addiction, wanting to die, inappropriately dealing with his anger, and lack of sexual interest.

Steve has not returned to jail for many years and has no plans of ever being incarcerated again. He is an active member in the community and volunteers for several organizations in town. In fact, he has been given awards for his commitment and dedication to his city.

He is alcohol and drug-free and enjoys his life with his wife. He no longer wishes to die and has had no suicide attempts. Steve attributes some of these changes to being able to express himself openly with others. He no longer struggles with inappropriate responses to anger.

His sex life is not as fulfilling as he would like, but he enjoys sexual interactions with his wife. Steve avoided sexuality throughout most of his life.

If you could say something to a man thinking about reaching out for help, what would that be?

- "Seek proper counselling."
- "Find the right roads, and keep looking until you do."
- "Do not go to doctors."
- "Be careful with medication."
- "DON'T GIVE UP."
- "If you give up and die, then other survivors lose."

Mark is in his late thirties and has never been married. He lived at home for the first thirty years of his life. Although he had several jobs throughout the group process, he was still unhappy with his employment situation.

The abuse

Mark described the communication between his family members as superficial and lacking any true emotional content. When he was younger, his friends and he would torment his father by stealing from him just to get him angry. His friends would ridicule his dad, and he joined them, hoping to be accepted by their group. Mark was embarrassed that his father was an alcoholic and could not speak English. They rarely talked to each other unless they were arguing.

When Mark was approximately seven, he was involved in sexual acts with his brothers, who were fourteen and sixteen at the time. He recalled incidents that included fondling, masturbation, and oral sex. Looking back, he remembers longing for love and attention. He did not know the sexual abuse was wrong. In fact, he thought it was positive and did not want it to end. Two years later, his siblings stopped approaching him, and he wondered why he no longer got this "special" attention from the brothers he wanted so desperately to have a relationship with. He started approaching his siblings in a sexual way and wanted everything to be like what he was accustomed to. His brothers got angry and refused his advances. Looking back, he thinks they realized their behaviour was inappropriate, but they didn't explain the process to him. He was left feeling as if he had done something wrong. Mark felt rejected and abandoned. When he was being abused by his brothers, everything felt fine. He hated them for ending the sexual attention and removing what he thought was love from them.

When he started viewing the sexual experiences as inappropriate, he became embarrassed and feared that others might find out. The shame he felt was enough motivation to keep quiet.

The effects

Mark talked about becoming totally introverted. He recalls "closing up" and not trusting anybody. Vulnerable feelings and negative self talk contributed to his low self-esteem. His inner voice was constantly reminding him to watch what he said or how he said it. He feared that others would find out about his past experiences. Finding ways to keep his thoughts from being exposed was not an easy task.

He masked his emptiness by experimenting with alcohol at the age of nine. As years passed by and alcohol became more readily available, he started using this coping skill on a regular basis to the point of alcoholism. Mark mentions being embarrassed with the things he would say and do while drunk. He talked about destroying his body with the booze and his mind with the blackouts. Mark remembered sniffing glue at the age of ten and how he is now concerned this may still have an effect on the way he thinks as an adult.

Connecting with friends and developing long-term relationships has been one of his struggles. In his younger years, he saw himself as a rebel with a big attitude, stating that he hated others and would harass people when given the opportunity.

When he quit drinking, he talked about helping others at his own expense, believing that by performing for others, he could make up for his past actions. He was scared to approach women that were interesting because of how he felt about himself. Asking for a dance at the local pub was out of the question, even if he was drunk. This created a situation where he settled for relationships that created more concerns for him than he needed. He talked about subconsciously looking for people that needed his help so that he would feel good about himself.

At times, he says he wanted too much attention from his friends. Mark talks about intimate relationships with past girlfriends and how they must have had similar misguided views about sexuality. He believed he had to have sex with them every night or they would leave him and find someone else. His worth was only as good as his performance in the bedroom. One girlfriend wanted to give him fellatio all the time, and he thought that contributed to the end of their relationship. It reminded him too much of his childhood.

Mark said masturbation had become a habit before the age of ten. Once the sexual interactions with his older brothers ended, he continually masturbated even though he was too young to ejaculate. This created shame, and he thought he was a bad person.

At the age of eleven, Mark and three friends had sexual intercourse with a sixteen-year-old girl that had a reputation for having many sexual partners. He talks about this event as being good for him. It felt good for him to participate in a sexual act with someone other than from his same gender. Even though his friends had no interest in this young lady, he felt a loss after this sexual relationship ended. Mark thinks this was another time that he confused sex with love.

When Mark got older, he would get drunk and let homosexual men take him home. After having sexual acts with them, he would steal their personal belongings. When he sobered up the next day, he would feel remorse for his actions. He remembers feeling a lot of shame and embarrassment for being with other men, and said that being homophobic did not help matters.

Mark talked about his struggles with being a "sex and love addict." He frequently picked up prostitutes to feed his obsessive/compulsive needs. He talked about this shameful activity as a way to stop the "inner chatter" in his mind. The compulsive act quieted the obsessive thought pattern. Mark thought he would never live past fifty, thinking he would contract a sexually transmitted disease and die.

Reaching out and rebuilding

Mark says he told various people about the abuse but not in a fashion that was productive for him. The first few times occurred while he was very drunk and crying his eyes out. The group he hung around with at that time was not interested in that type of discussion.

The next time he mentioned the sexual abuse was when he was in a recovery home for alcoholism. Even though it was discussed, it didn't seem to help. Looking into the effects of being sexually abused was not what Mark wanted; he just wanted to get out of rehabilitation and continue drinking.

He mentioned that he confided in four girlfriends over the years but not because he wanted to deal with the past; he just wanted to provide an excuse for his behaviour. Mark said the "poor me" comments got him off the hook, along with receiving some desired attention.

Mark confronted his oldest sibling on three or four occasions when drunk. Sometimes he would tell his older brother's girlfriends in an attempt to get even. Unfortunately, the personal problems he was having in his life made others feel he was not credible, and nobody believed him.

Alcoholic's Anonymous meetings created a safe atmosphere where he was able to share parts of his past with fellow group members. Mark commented it was helpful, but he never connected the abuse to the totality of everything that was happening around him.

A sponsor from "AA" was the first person Mark remembers telling in a non-subtle, serious way. This person encouraged him to seek help from someone that had direct knowledge of male sexual abuse recovery.

Requesting services from a counsellor was not easy. He was hesitant because he did not think he could trust anyone who he believed got paid to care about others. He thought that any counsellor who receives money for caring must have a self-serving agenda.

After eight months of individual counselling, combined with Mark's positive experiences with "AA" groups, he decided to join a support group for male sexual abuse survivors.

Five years later

How were support groups helpful?

- "It felt good to share."
- "I also had many "AA" meetings to go to."
- "Developing new friendships was nice."
- "It gave me a sense that everything was going to be okay."

Although Mark found group to be beneficial, he preferred the "AA" style of meeting where there was less structure and more opportunity to attend sessions at various times of the day. He regrets that he missed some meetings and wished there were less topics covered over a short period of time.

Are you in a better place now? How are you different compared to when you first reached out for help?

- "The removal of shame has given me more free energy."
- "I am more humble now and do not have to project any image other than who I am."
- "I am more comfortable in my own skin."
- "I have become aware of myself, and I have an understanding of how I relate to others."
- "I am not so gullible and cannot be conned so easily by others."
- "It feels good to take my time and have more patience."

- "I do not give as freely as I used to; I do not fall in love right away."
- "I've seen the light."
- "I have learned to meet my own needs."
- "I am not so critical; there is calm amongst the storm of life. There are normal stressful situations happening in my life, but I'm not as fearful or erratic in how I respond to stress."
- "I am more peaceful with myself."
- "I stay at home more and am more comfortable being alone."
- "I enjoy both life and work more."
- "I'm not as resentful as I was before, and when I do become resentful, it passes."
- "I am not as materialistic as I was before and have a better understanding of myself."
- "The hurts and pains have subsided."
- "I still have pain, but it is not as intense; my emotions connected to the past are not triggered as easily. When they do come up, I know how to deal with them, and they do not last as long."

Mark mentioned the effects of the abuse included: abusing alcohol, being unhappy with his employment situation, Mark has been alcohol and drug-free for the past five years. He is gainfully employed and is happy with his present position. His inappropriate responses to anger from the past have subsided, and he talks about his feelings and emotions openly.

There were times in the past when Mark talked about being grandiose at one moment and filled with shame and regret the rest of the time. He is now more peaceful with himself and has learned to be comfortable in his own skin.

Getting rid of his attitude from the past has given him more confidence when interacting and having empathy for others. Although he still struggles at times with his sexuality, he has made great progress in understanding and modifying his behaviour.

If you could say something to a man thinking about reaching out for help, what would that be?

- "I do not like to give advice."
- "Recovery is definitely worth it and better than the price you pay in hiding."
- "Keep the faith and keep it simple."

Fred's Story

Fred is a man in his early thirties. He has lived with his parents all his life. At the time group began, he feared relationships and had never been married. He was unemployed throughout the group process.

The abuse

Fred talks about having a good family upbringing but regrets the lack of open expression between him and his parents. Living at home seemed adequate at the moment, but he hoped to find a place of his own someday.

His first sexual experience occurred at the young age of six, when a fourteen-year-old male cousin enticed him into acts that included masturbation and fondling. This was a one-time occurrence.

At the age of eight, Fred remembers enjoying the company of his eighteen-year-old male babysitter. This person was not seen as just a babysitter, but a special, older friend. Over a period of two months, this caregiver coerced this child into acts of touching and masturbation. Fred stated he was too young to understand exactly what was happening, and he wasn't mature enough to realize the sexual acts were wrong or abusive.

The babysitter made it very clear that Fred was not to tell his mom or he would lose their friendship. The last thing Fred wanted was to betray this person's trust. Years passed by before Fred realized he was the one who had been betrayed, and it was his own trust that had been violated.

When Fred recognized the abuse was affecting him, he felt unable to reach out and break silence. He had feelings of embarrassment, thinking he was responsible for the abuse. Fred mentions not wanting his parents to be ashamed of him. He was concerned that if others knew, they would consider him a "fag." The thought of being rejected and ridiculed by others was enough motivation to struggle alone.

The effects

Puberty became a lonely time as Fred continued to suppress his feelings connected to the past sexual abuse.

He had low self-esteem and was scared of everything around him. Fred isolated himself in the house and refused to interact with the other boys in the neighbourhood. Television became his best friend, watching it from the moment he woke up until the time he went to bed. The next day, he would repeat the same pattern.

The emptiness inside him seemed bottomless, and overeating filled a portion of that void. Food helped him to keep his mind off the abuse. Due to lack of activity, and suppressing his feelings with food, he became overweight. This escalated over the years, and Fred became more and more depressed. The more depressed he got, the more he ate. The more he ate, the worse he felt about himself. The worse he felt about himself, the more he ate. He repeated this vicious cycle for many years.

Entering into adulthood was a difficult transition filled with many irritable moments and mood swings. At one moment, he was calm, and the next, he was totally miserable, without any apparent awareness of the abrupt changes. Anger became an unpredictable part of his daily life.

The topic of healthy sexuality was very frightening for Fred. Although he never questioned his sexual preference, thoughts of the past left him with a mental image that he was a "pervert." Curiosity about pornography reinforced to him what a bad person he was.

In his twenties, he desperately wanted to date, but a negative view of himself left him feeling that nobody from the opposite sex would ever find him attractive or desirable. Negative self-worth combined with a fear of rejection created an atmosphere where it seemed easier to stay alone and be depressed. He would tell himself that he was unlovable and destined to be alone forever. He did not like the thought of not having a girlfriend, but his fears of rejection hindered him from reaching out. He put his sexuality on hold until his thirties.

Reaching out and rebuilding

Fifteen years after the abuse took place, a female cousin said that she was sexually abused by the same person who victimized him. They had a number of conversations, and it felt good to break silence and talk about his troubling past. She was a good listener who gave him sound advice. His cousin was benefiting from individual counselling at the local Sexual Assault Crisis Centre and encouraged him to do the same.

Six months later, he phoned the Crisis Centre and made his first appointment. Telling another man about the past made him feel like a huge weight had been lifted off his shoulders. Fred attended individual counselling for several years before joining a support group for male sexual abuse survivors on his counsellor's recommendation.

Five years later

How were support groups helpful?

- "I didn't feel alone."
- "It was nice to make new friends."

- "Helping others made me feel better about myself."
- "I did not feel like the odd one anymore."
- "It may sound like an odd comment, but it made me realize that other people may have it worse than I do, and if they can work through their problems, then so can I."
- "Group was excellent for the healing process."

Fred felt that support groups were a good option for him after receiving individual counselling. It helped him to overcome his shyness and reach out to others. Being validated by others was a confidence booster that helped with life outside of group.

Are you in a better place now? How are you different compared to when you first reached out for help?

- "I have come out of my shell."
- "It has opened me up."
- "I became more confident in approaching women."
- "I learned to love myself, and as a result, I can love others more."
- "I am more outgoing and enjoy going out into the world. It is not the scary place I once thought it was."
- "I realized that not all people are bad and some are even trustworthy.
- "I am proud of how I handled my recovery process."

- "I have not forgiven the abuser, but I have come to an acceptance that he had a problem that caused him to pick up some bad habits along the way."
- "Even though recovering from the abuse was hard, I am a better person. This negative situation turned me into a better person."
- "I stop and notice the beauty around me now. Before, I was scared to leave my home; now I love to see the outdoors."

Fred mentioned several concerns including: being unemployed, not being able to find a date, lack of activity, overeating, suppressing feelings, and concerns with anger.

He is now gainfully employed and owns his own business. His girlfriend describes him as the most kind, gentle man she has ever met. They are discussing options of moving in together in the near future.

Fred works out at the local gym on a regular basis and has become an expert on nutrition and exercise. He speaks openly about his feelings and emotions and handles his anger very respectfully.

If you could say something to a man thinking about reaching out for help, what would that be?

- "Talk to someone as soon as you can find a safe opportunity."
- "Two heads are better than one."
- "Find professional help."

- "Talk to someone who is not emotionally connected to the situation."
- "Talk to someone that is educated on sexual abuse recovery."
- "I strongly recommend individual counselling and then group."

Matthew was thirty-one, single, with no children at the time he joined the support group. He was employed but unhappy with his attempts to upgrade his educational skills in hopes of increasing his potential for better employment opportunities.

The abuse

Matthew describes his childhood as a dysfunctional environment that was not conducive to healthy role modelling. His family was poor, and they struggled to get by from day to day. When he was under the age of ten, his mother would bring men home from the bar while his dad was at work. He witnessed her engaging in sexual acts with these people on several occasions. Matthew "carried" a lot of embarrassment about his family's lifestyle, and he did not want others to associate him with them.

Between the ages of eight to ten, Matthew was lured into the home of a fifty-year-old neighbourhood man who would give him money. Matthew explained that horrible things happened to him as a small boy in that house, including masturbation and anal intercourse. At the time, he trusted this man and he felt good about receiving money.

He kept silent about the abuse for fear of being ridiculed and didn't want others to look badly upon him. He felt a lot of shame about exchanging sexual favours for money.

The effects

Matthew talked about how his feelings of low self-worth turned into depression. He was angry at himself for the situation with the neighbourhood man and mad that he did not get it out in the open sooner. He says it was a secret that should have been told. Matthew explained that he got fed up with life and started living "on the edge," flirting with danger and risky behaviours as a way to cope with his emotional needs.

He is a highly-motivated individual who is articulate and well-educated on issues pertaining to human behaviour. Like many survivors, he looks back with remorse on how he responded to his childhood experiences.

Matthew recognizes his talents and feels he was an underachiever. He talked about a whole series of self-destructive behaviours and poor decision-making, citing lost opportunities with poor career choices. In particular, he had a well-paying government position with a future, but he quit. He always knew he had lots of potential and lots of ability, but he thought the job was causing him pain, when in fact, he was haunted by memories from the past.

He explained that his problems always appeared to be something "outside" of himself and how he operated from the outside-in compared to the inside-out. Whenever he was in pain, he would look outside of himself for the reason, thinking it was his job, his partner, or something else, never realizing that the pain was coming from within.

Relationships were a big concern for Matthew. He was attracted to partners who he thought would make him feel good about who he was. He longed for praise from them in order to maintain his self-esteem. A pattern of co-dependant relationships developed, in which he would eagerly attempt to meet his partners' needs at his own expense. Matthew thought that if he could make them happy, then he would be happy.

Many of his relationships were based on sexual performance. He thought his worth as a partner evolved around how good he was in bed. Their interactions were more sexual than intimate. Sex was the main determining factor in evaluating if a relationship was good or worth continuing.

Reaching out and rebuilding

The first time he talked about being sexually abused was twenty years after the neighbourhood man victimized him. As an adult, he mentioned the abuse briefly in a counselling session dealing with relationship concerns. He never went back to that counsellor.

The next time he talked about the abuse was with a girlfriend who had been sexually traumatized herself. She was in the process of legal proceedings against her abuser. He shared his story in a non-feeling, matter-of-fact fashion.

Two years later, he spoke to a friend from his Al-Anon group. His buddy was having similar concerns with his partner and suggested it may be worth it for Matthew to explore the possible links between childhood sexual abuse and his problems with relationships. His friend had dealt with his own victimization and recommended the Sexual Assault Crisis Centre.

Even though Matthew went to the Sexual Assault Crisis Centre with a specific agenda to work on relationships, he talked about individual counselling as a life awareness tool for him. He was surprised how the sexual abuse was linked to many other problem areas of his life. After two years of individual counselling, Matthew took advantage of the opportunity to join a support group.

Five years later

How were support groups helpful?

- "I did not feel alone or isolated."
- "These were real live people with the same thoughts and fears."
- "It was a safe atmosphere for one to express how they feel, and a place to gain an awareness of self."
- "A mirroring process takes place where you can see yourself in other people's comments."

- "I could relate to others' experiences and relate it to my own life."
- "It helped me to better understand my feelings."
- "It was a safer atmosphere than most available places. You generally do not share these concerns with anybody. The group allows you to trust others and yourself."

Although Matthew had worked through most of his recovery issues in individual counselling, the group experience enhanced his growth.

Are you in a better place now? How are you different compared to when you first reached out for help?

- "I have lots of self awareness."
- "I still have a lot of fears."
- "Where I am now is a much better place; it seems like a million years ago that I was working on issues. It was necessary but horrible back then."
- "I don't depend on others for self-worth or to give me self-esteem."
- "I have an acceptance of my weaknesses and strengths."
- "Although I could live alone, I prefer someone with me."
- "I am not the social butterfly or feel I have to be one like I once thought."
- "I am confident now it was not my fault."
- "My relationships with my partner and others are much more stable."

- "I am more able to define my needs and comfortable finding solutions to these needs."
- "I have an awareness that some of my characteristics are genetic, and I have to live with that."
- "I am able to look at the whole package (me), and I am comfortable with that."

When Matthew started his recovery process, he was concerned with: upgrading his educational skills, unhealthy relationships based mainly on sex, feelings of remorse, embarrassment about family, working from the outside-in, and pre-occupied with thoughts of the past.

Matthew is gainfully employed and is working hard at taking college courses at the same time. He has been in a stable interdependent relationship for the past four years, which is based on open communication and respect.

He no longer feels remorse or shame about himself or his family of origin. Operating from the inside-out has brought him to a much better place, where he connects with both himself and those around him. Matthew laughs when stating it seems like a million years ago he was working on sexual abuse related concerns.

If you could say something to a man thinking about reaching out for help, what would that be?

- "Don't just go to any counsellor. Go to someone who deals specifically with sexual abuse recovery, or at least someone with a strong background in it."

- "I would encourage them to talk about it."
- "Deal with the issues, now, before they escalate into problems and behaviours that will create more concerns for you later."
- "Seek help as soon as possible."
- "Too many men wait until they hit bottom because they have too many fears connected to taking an honest look in the mirror."
- "There is probably something in your behaviours related to sexual abuse that you are not even aware of."
- "If you are not aware that your behaviours are harmful to you, then you will not deal with them. If you refuse to take an honest look at yourself, you won't deal with it."
- "Until you feel it, you won't deal with it."

The men from group were very happy to be interviewed five years after the first group took place. They were thankful to be part of a positive growing experience and hope that their efforts will add to your learning experience.

Part #2

Stages of Recovery

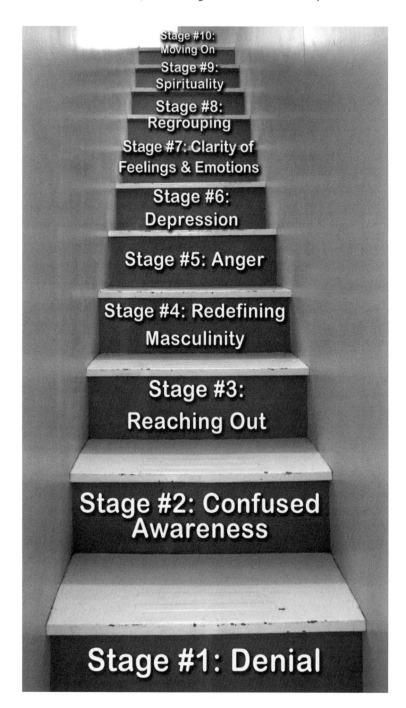

Stage #10:
Moving On

Stage #9:
Spirituality

Stage #8:
Regrouping

Stage #7: Clarity of
Feelings & Emotions

Stage #6:
Depression

Stage #5: Anger

Stage #4: Redefining
Masculinity

Stage #3:
Reaching Out

Stage #2: Confused
Awareness

Stage #1: Denial

Many men who were sexually victimized as children find themselves faced with a perplexing challenge as an adult. The skills they used as a child tend to be counter productive as an adult. The perils of silence became more painful than the risks of transforming and healing.

Outlining the stages of recovery can be a misleading message to someone who is looking for a systematic, definitive plan that specifically tells them what their journey will entail. Every individual's recovery process is unique; no two are identical. However, most journeys have commonalities. The ten stages of recovery outlined here may give you an overview of what some men have experienced in their pilgrimage towards wholeness. Healing is not linear; it is back and forth and all over the place, resembling an upwardly spiralling design moving towards a destination determined by the individual. It can also be like a spider web that has many connections travelling in differing directions. Each person has a different web and follows a different path. People can be in various stages, or dealing with several of them at the same time. A person can be at one stage in one aspect of their lives and at a completely different stage in other areas.

The stages outlined here can help people design their own plan, based on the experience of others. This model typifies the journey of most but not all men. This is a brief summary and these topics will be expanded upon later in this book.

Stage #1: Denial

It is not unusual for people to be trapped in this stage for many years after the physical nature of the abuse has ended. There are many good, valid reasons why denial exists and persists. Resurfacing "ghosts" from the past is not easy to deal with. Even though the mind suppressed these memories for a good reason, there is a cost involved with keeping unresolved issues away from conscious awareness. Denial, whether it is conscious or subconscious, takes up a lot of emotional energy. Men talk about stuffing or burying feelings through the overuse of alcohol, chemical substances, prescribed medications, and other addictions.

These men were concerned about their inability to trust anyone, including themselves. Control can become a key concern for many men. They often find themselves in one of two extremes: either they feel totally controlled by others, or they try to totally control themselves and everything around them.

Having a positive connection with themselves and others seems unattainable for many sexually abused men. Due to the lack of educational material and health programs available for male survivors, many men choose secrecy and isolation until life becomes unmanageable. Others stay in denial forever, choosing to live with the associated costs involved with keeping the "ghosts" from the past in the closet.

There is a big difference between privacy and denial. When someone is in denial they are not attending to concerns that are affecting their quality of life. However, everyone has the right to privacy and the choice of how they work through issues in their lives.

The single biggest concern that survivors express is the inability to connect with themselves and others. By staying in denial and creating a false self, they limit the healthy connection they so desperately desire. When men step out of denial and start to acknowledge how childhood sexual abuse has had an impact on their adult lives, they enter stage two.

Stage #2: Confused awareness

This is the point when men start to take an honest look at themselves. For years, they have tried to forget all uncomfortable memories without success.

Many men are jolted into disclosure for various reasons. When men are emotionally overloaded with feelings connected to a present event, it becomes much harder to keep feelings connected to the past at bay. It is not easy to face the past, but most people start this stage when overloaded with other concerns, and especially when seeing the connection between the pain from the past and the hurt in the present. Perhaps a marriage has failed or they are having difficulty relating to others. Maybe the perpetrator has passed away and they feel it is safer to speak. Addictions may be destroying connections with people or things they love. This new awareness puts them into shock as they experience anxiety, panic and fear. When beginning to deal with unwanted memories, people become confused, doubting their own perceptions.

There are a lot of inner negotiations going on at this stage, and some men wish they could just forget and move on. But once "the cat is out of the bag," it is much harder to stuff it back in. When people are emotionally overwhelmed, they either engage more heavily in old habits or make a decision to heal. A decision to heal brings men to the next stage.

Stage #3: Reaching out

Coming out of a fog is not easy when you are unsure what is on the other side. At this stage, men understand the abuse happened, but they also struggle with inner shame and embarrassment. Finding someone safe and supportive to tell their stories to is not an easy task. If people are fortunate enough to connect with someone supportive, a decrease of guilt and shame will result. Unfortunately, many men seek or get advice from someone who minimizes their pain and promotes an approach that puts men back into denial. One common damaging statement victims hear is "that happened a long time ago, so just forget about it." If it were that easy, they would have. Besides, they already tried that approach, and it did not work. Reaching out and telling their stories helps men define their core issues, along with identifying losses.

Once men step out of their "cocoon" and begin sorting through the feelings and emotions connected to the past, they often enter the next stage.

Stage #4: Defining masculinity

Most men would like to grieve from a purely intellectual perspective, but healing emotional wounds from the past means feelings must be processed and included. How men view masculinity will either hinder or enhance their journey. There are many myths surrounding being a man that are simply obstacles in the recovery path. If people feel that "real" men are not victims, then they often view themselves as not being "real" men.

This stage gives men an opportunity to become real. It allows a man to become a person who is free to explore a wide range of feelings and emotions. Vulnerability and reaching out for help can be viewed as masculine, as a strength and not a weakness. Often, this is when men start to realize the abusive situation was not their fault and they step into the next stage at full speed.

Stage #5: Anger

This is a stage of explosive feelings; it creates anger, rage, and a desire for justice. Disclosures and confrontations seem to preoccupy the thought process. Reaching this stage is a reason for celebration, but watch out for the fireworks. Group members talk of an intense, highly charged energy that can spark rage and vengeful thoughts. They are standing up to abuse and no longer want any part of the trauma bond that may be keeping them connected with the abuser. Anger is like gasoline. If used wisely, it will drive you to where you need to go. If used unwisely, it could blow up in your face.

Anger is an emotion that is essential to the healing process. People often confuse anger with behaviour, particularly when people respond to anger with violence. It is not anger that determines the healthiness of one's choices, it is the behaviour, or how one responds to anger, that determines if anger works for or against a person. Once someone works through their anger, they will enter the next challenging stage. Nobody wants to go there, but it is an integral part of the growth process.

Stage #6: Depression

When men speak out, they are in a process of intense growth. For this new growth to happen, they often give up portions of their "old-self." Behaviours that may have worked for them as children may hinder their quality of life as an adult. The coping skills that were once useful may be outdated and counter productive. Old patterns are not always healthy, but they are familiar, and a natural reaction to giving up old and familiar ways of living is depression. If depression helps people recognize the parts of their lives that need adjusting, then there can be a healthy component to this process.

This stage is a time of transformation and integration that brings all the parts of the person together. Throughout this stage, there seems to be a death of the old "self" and a birth of a newer, healthier self. Although this is an intense period of positive growth, it can be filled with feelings of helplessness, guilt, remorse, and despair. This stage includes grieving a loss that can leave someone feeling a great sense of emptiness and sadness.

Men in this stage often find themselves giving up a need for control. This is only a stage and it will help pave the way to a better place. This next stage can be an eye opener that will positively change people's lives forever.

Stage #7: Clarifying feelings and emotions

This stage is closely linked to the stage of depression. By gaining clarity to feelings and emotions, men are automatically working through other core issues that have plagued them for years. The more people process their feelings, the more they step out of depression. This is a wonderful, struggling, confusing, and insightful stage that helps men to come in contact with the hurt inner child they left behind. Grieving losses from the past helps facilitate learning that will help people grieve present day losses as they occur. Many men have not learned to acknowledge or identify the wide range of feelings and emotions that we all experience. This growing period usually requires help from someone outside their present environment, possibly individual counselling or a support group. Clarifying feelings and emotions is an integral part of the healing process, but it is especially useful when stepping out of depression and into the next stage.

Stage #8: Regrouping

Although all stages are important, this is the phase that entails a lot of hope. Regrouping is a transforming stage, where people start learning to trust appropriately, and most importantly, they learn to trust themselves. They are developing skills to assist them in getting their needs met in a healthy fashion. By taking responsibility for their lives they feel empowered, with enhanced feelings of self worth.

People have worked very hard to get to this point and are starting to like the new person they have become. They are learning to <u>find their own voice</u>. A voice that is able to speak their truth. In the previous stages, group members would characterize themselves as existing and not living. This stage is a time when the search for meaning is fuelled by a desire to live life. Many victims do not plan for a future because they never thought there would be one; others expected to die young. Regrouping includes putting joy into the journeys.

Redefining friendships leads to improved intimacy and love. Loneliness is converted into enjoying their own company and being comfortable with themselves. This great stage opens a person up to a new world full of opportunity.

The next stage is a process that many people are hesitant to talk about, but from my experience, when some people reach this point, their recovery seems to take off at a speed that can only be called miraculous.

Stage #9: Spirituality

As many people grow and mature through the stages, they get a sense of power within themselves that is also greater than themselves. Some group members say it is like describing the indescribable. A sense of inner peace is connected to what can be viewed as "true reality." They talk about an emptiness lifting, and they feel they will never feel alone again. This spiritual connection is often viewed as unconditional love and acceptance.

Some men have concerns that others are more advanced in their spiritual beliefs than they are. Where people are spiritually, at any given point in time, is exactly where they should be. Spirituality is an individual, experiential journey that develops over time. It is a process, and as people work through their recovery, their views on spirituality often change. A person does not have to be spiritual to heal. RYHSR groups are based on the principle that people have the right to establish their own spirituality and beliefs.

Men often talk about the healing powers of forgiveness at this stage. People do not have to forgive the abuser in order to heal, but it is important to forgive themselves. For a more in-depth look at forgiveness, please read the chapter on spirituality.

People who have travelled this far have fought a long, strenuous, rewarding journey. Finally it is time to enter the last stage.

Stage #10: Moving on

This stage includes the rest of their lives. It would be unfair to think people become "home free" and will never feel vulnerable again. In fact, many men go back and refine some of the stages at some time in their lives. How someone views their abusive experience changes from a subjective experience to an objective experience. The thought process becomes more objective than subjective. They have memories that exist independently of painful feelings and emotions.

This stage is a much more comfortable place, which includes deep and lasting changes with a sense of stability. If people seek help to improve their connection with themselves, others, and the world they live in, then moving-on must include maintaining the connections they desire.

Stage # 1: Denial

Denial can be a defence mechanism that is used in an attempt to reduce anxiety by denying thoughts, feelings, or facts that may seem to be intolerable. Every person has a right to privacy, but denial can be a costly way of avoiding the truth. Wearing a mask to hide feelings and emotions can be a way of protecting oneself from pain and suffering, in addition to portraying oneself as "normal."

Men in sexual abuse support groups are grieving from trauma that took place many years prior to reaching out. A child's body seems to have its own built-in safety mechanism that shuts down when overloaded. When trauma is too severe, the mind and body will suppress, repress, and disassociate memories until a time when it is safer for them to surface. The body goes into shock to protect itself, cocooning itself in order to survive. This shock often lasts for many years. There are many good reasons why people wait until a time and place in their lives when it may be safer to deal with unresolved issues from the past.

Why do men wait so long before seeking help?

- "Part of me felt it was my fault."
- "I was too young. I was not sure how I felt about it."
- "I felt shame whenever I thought about the situation."
- "At the time, I did not know a woman could sexually abuse boys."
- "I did not realize it was abuse. I thought I was being introduced to sex."

- "The abuser led me to believe this type of activity was normal."
- "I thought only women could be sexually abused."
- "Abusers are master manipulators; they know how to keep you silent."
- "I was not ready to talk about it, and I did not think anyone would believe me."
- "I received very clear messages from family, friends, and society. My role was to keep silent. Parents can be very persuasive when you are young."
- "I did not have a voice, and when I tried to talk about it, nobody would listen."
- "Just the thought of telling some else was too scary; I was afraid."
- "Society was not ready. They do not accept men as victims."
- "I thought people would think I was gay."
- "There was no safe place to go, and there was no help available."
- "I felt all alone; nobody would accept me if I told."
- "If I let the rage out, I would have probably killed somebody. I could not take that chance. My rage was too strong."
- "There was never a right time to talk about the sexual abuse."
- "I could not devalue the family name and risk my mom having a heart attack."
- "I had to wait for certain family members to die before it was safe enough to talk."
- "I felt that my body betrayed me; part of me enjoyed the abuse."

All group participants wished they had come forward sooner and dealt with the victimization they experienced as children. There were many good, valid reasons why these men waited to talk about their pasts. The reality is they could not have come forward one moment sooner. The time was not right for whatever reason, and these men are exactly where they should be in their recovery processes. Both survivors and their support teams need to honour this. There is no need for self-blame on behalf of the victim, and the last thing anyone needs is to be judged by others.

It takes a lot of emotional energy to keep memories from the past sealed within the body. These memories attempt to surface at different points in time and the skills used to push them back into silence can be unhealthy. As time evolves, people tend to become more conscious of what their bodies are trying to tell them. Thus, they enter into a state of confused awareness.

Stage #2: Confused Awareness

Memories connected to sexual abuse experiences are often frozen in time, kept tightly concealed within the body and he mind. As time evolves, these memories begin to defrost and surface on a more conscious level. This gives victims an opportunity to either explore and express them, or find further ways to suppress them. Even though victims suffered alone as a child, they do not have to suffer alone as adults. They now have people who want to help them. Participants often talk about the negative coping skills they used to suppress their past memories. These coping skills seemed negative in the past, but it kept them alive and allowed them to survive, getting them to where they are right now; and that is exactly where they should be.

This stage of recovery is about gaining insight into old belief patterns and entertaining the thought of developing new ways of coping. When the pain of secrecy and isolation are greater than the perceived pain of moving forward, a transition tends to take place.

People become aware that coping skills that were effective as a child are no longer useful as an adult. Secrecy, isolation, and denial may have seemed like a safe place, however, the "ghosts" from the past keep wanting to resurface. Victims may have learned that not expressing themselves helped them to cope with their childhood family, but this may not be effective in their adult relationships.

Participants looked back in time and said they would have this inner conflict and would often trick themselves into remaining stuck by using coping skills such as: overeating, addictions to drugs, alcohol, shopping, sex, avoiding relationships, and isolation. The chronic mistrust in others, combined with minimizing their pain, continued to keep them in confusion. These brave men wondered if they were strong enough to admit they needed help, yet, they were unable to resolve their problems on their own.

Participants said they had many fears that hindered them from reaching out. If they were to let the "cat out of the bag," it would be difficult to return to a state of denial. Once they reached out, it would not be easy to return to their old coping skills.

What fears hinder someone from talking about the abuse they experienced?

- **"Fear** of losing control."
- **"Fear** of being too feminine."
- **"Fear** of hurting others."
- **"Fear** that I will be rejected by the person I am talking to."
- **"Fear** of abandonment; will this person leave me?"

Survivors need a lot of courage to remove the masks they hid behind. Pretending to be strong served a purpose, but it blocked them from their true feelings and emotions. It also drained them of the necessary energy needed to overcome their fears. Until people can see the value in change they will remain living with the skills that are familiar to them. Even if these skills are unhealthy, they are familiar.

Stage #3: Reaching Out

Reaching out and asking for help can be a humbling experience. This chapter focuses on discussions about individual and group counselling. Men talk about making that first dreaded call and showing up for their first appointment. Some of them were jolted into disclosure, while others wished they had reached out sooner. Participants will share the different qualities they look for in a counsellor.

Lastly, men talk about how they benefited from individual counselling.

The first call for help can be a tension-filled experience. One group member said he considered calling the office for months, but could not bring himself to dial the number. One day, he found the courage and made the call. Upon hearing a voice on the other end of the line, he froze and hung up immediately. Several months passed before he gathered enough strength to try again. This time he was determined to speak, only to hang up another time. After one year, he made another call and engaged in a conversation. A thirty minute discussion took place, and he decided to schedule an appointment.

It is common for survivors to be ambivalent when stepping away from the perceived safety of secrecy and isolation. Participants said they had the illusion that silence is their protection. But, by coming out and talking about the past, they were standing up against the abuse. This gave them a sense of personal power that they had not felt previously.

The next hurdle was showing up for the first counselling appointment. This is their most difficult session to attend. Men said they confronted a wide variety of fears when preparing to attend that first appointment. Several men parked their cars a few blocks away from the office, even though spots were available close to the building. They feared somebody might see their automobile parked at a "Sexual Assault Crisis Centre" and conclude that they were sexual abuse survivors. Some folks scheduled evening appointments when it would be dark outside, and they attempted to slip in the side door unnoticed. After several sessions they became more at ease with the situation.

One group member talked about his first appointment — even though he did not know me, he said he did not like me; he did not want to be there; and he did not want to talk to me. He was bitter that he was having problems at home and did not think talking to another man would help. Interestingly enough, he mentioned that when he pried the words out, he was relieved that he talked to another man. He was especially happy that someone was genuinely interested in hearing his story without taking advantage of his vulnerability.

Another participant said he was very hesitant when showing up for his first appointment. His inner voice told him not to trust any counsellor who gets paid to talk with people. He was concerned about confidentiality, thinking his comments would be talked about in the community. This man thought all full-time counsellors must have a hidden agenda that was self-serving. He made a valid point about his fears at that time, stating, "If you can't trust family and friends, how can you be expected to trust a stranger?" As time evolved, he became more comfortable and a trusting counsellor/survivor relationship developed.

Many people who seek individual counselling may not be ready to join a group. Others seek help in the third person, wanting education and help regarding loved ones who have been abused. One person sought help for a situation that involved his sister. He wanted to know everything he could about sexual abuse recovery without being able to talk about his own abusive situation. He attended counselling for some time before he disclosed the circumstances of his own victimization.

Group members talked about being jolted into disclosure, feeling they had to hit "rock bottom" before requesting counselling. Something traumatic had happened in their lives to jar them into talking about their pain from the past. They could not contain their feelings and emotions connected to a stressful situation in the present, and at the same time, keep others buried from the past. They mentioned being jolted by a potential divorce, chemical addictions, trouble with the law, relationship problems, sexual addictions, and other overwhelming triggers. Far too many men wait until they are hospitalized with nervous breakdowns or attempted suicides before they reach out. Too many men kill themselves without seeking or finding help. A network of male support services could provide safe help before men "hit bottom" and thus reduce the high rate of male suicide.

Finding a counsellor that specializes in male sexual abuse recovery issues can be like finding a "needle in the haystack." These men listed the qualities they prefer in a counsellor.

When choosing a counsellor, what qualities do you look for?

- "I have to feel safe and comfortable."
- "Shop around and find somebody you are comfortable with."
- "Their attitude is important. I do not want them to be aloof."
- "He has to be educated on male sexual abuse issues."
- "I do not like to go places that immediately push drugs on you."
- "Posture is very important to me. If I go into the counselling session, the counsellor must appear to be interested in my story."
- "There has to be eye contact."
- "If he yawns, leave."
- "Listening skills are the most important."
- "The counsellor has to be male."
- "If there is a desk between me and the counsellor, I feel like there is a barrier."
- "I have to be at the same level as the counsellor. Although I respect that I am the client, I am an equal as a person."
- "We need to do our own growth; the counsellor must respect this and not be too rigid in his approach."

- "I do not want to be analyzed. I do not want the counsellor to figure me out. They have to allow me to grow on my own."
- "I do not want to be told what to do."
- "Go see someone who promotes self-empowerment."
- "Education and insight has to be passed on in a respectful manner. I need someone that will help me explore my options."

The men in group talked about needing to trust one person before they felt comfortable trusting others. Several people commented that until they were ready, they would have rather died than tell anyone about the sexual abuse. They expressed the importance of finding safe and supportive people when reaching out, especially in the beginning when they were the most vulnerable. Several participants mentioned how negative responses from others sent them back into silence for years.

How did you personally benefit from individual counselling?

- "It seemed like a big weight had been lifted off my shoulders."
- "I always believed the abuse was my fault. I learned that I was not the problem and it was not my fault."
- "It helped to remove the shame I was carrying around."
- "If I did not get individual counselling, I would be dead."
- "I got another chance at life."

- "It felt nice that others cared, finally someone cared."
- "The different slogans and metaphors used are something I carry around with me daily."
- "Counselling helped me to open up, which gave clarity to my thoughts and feelings."
- "Even though I went for the specific reason of working on relationships, it became a life awareness tool for me. It was a worthwhile discovery and journey."
- "Counselling helped me to define reality."
- "I gained new skills that I did not have before."
- "Counselling helped me to channel insight and awareness. It was important for someone to help me put it all together. Getting a second opinion was beneficial."
- "Everything about counselling was positive."
- "Individual counselling was a good stepping stone to group."

After individual counselling, support groups are the next logical step, a place where men can reach out to others and be supported by people with similar experiences.

Joining a survivor support group

Joining a support group for the first time can be very intimidating. One man questioned how he could tell his fellow participants that he performed fellatio on his minister for six years. It was hard enough for him to share this in individual counselling let alone with a group of strangers. By joining this group, he would be re-experiencing the pain connected to this childhood experience, along with digging up other unwanted memories. He knew it would be impossible to hide his pain throughout the ten week program. The decision to join the group was a tremendous risk.

The decision was no easier for another group member, who at the age of twelve was sexually abused by two seventeen-year-old female babysitters. He never understood it was sexual abuse until later in life. His friends gave him the impression he was a "real stud" for "scoring" at a young age, thinking he should be happy about such an opportunity. Not until he was in his thirties did he realize the damaging effects the abuse had had on him and his views of women. He questioned how he could talk about something that was so harmful, when others may think he was lucky. He wondered if he would be supported or laughed at.

By addressing fears and taking risks, they knew they would be exposing their deepest, darkest secrets to the others and wondered how they would be perceived. Would other group members judge them? What if they felt like crying? What if they did cry? What if they fell apart; would their pain be minimized? Would these other men accept them at their most vulnerable moment? Would the sharing of personal information be too intimidating in front of strangers? Would disclosure lead to humiliation, further pain, and sadness? Did they want to risk the chance that other participants may break confidentiality and mention details of their abuse outside the group meeting room? Was it possible that something that seemed so frightening could actually be helpful? It was good for these men to talk about their fears in individual counselling before entering a support group. Some men still had these fears when group began but they worked through them with each other.

Not all group members are intimidated or frightened when entering group. Some men looked forward to their group experience, especially those who had positive experiences from other groups such as Alcoholics Anonymous. Other men took part in individual counselling for extended periods of time when no sexual abuse support groups were being offered. When the opportunity presented itself to become part of a group, most of them gladly accepted.

Group was a natural, logical progression for participants, and it became an integral part of their healing journey. As they grew and evolved as individuals in the counselling room, they longed to be part of something greater. Joining a group became the next logical place for new growth, a place where they were accepted and supported by their peers. Members acknowledged that group was a stepping stone to another place, a place of having positive connections in the greater context of their communities.

What do you hope to gain from your group experience?

- "Sharing with each other."
- "Support from the group."
- "I would like to learn from each other."
- "I would like to get in touch with myself."
- "Eventually, I would like to educate others in the community."

- "Establish trust."
- "I'll feel it out as the group progresses."
- "Get acceptance for who I am."

The group experience gave these men an opportunity to learn more about themselves. They had an opportunity to identify their needs and ask others about alternative ways of getting these needs met. It also gave them an opportunity to expand on their support team by developing new friendships and enlarging their circle of trust.

Many men were afraid to be open and honest about themselves, fearing their comments would hurt them personally, or someone else. With practice, some participants learned to resolve conflict non-violently, while others learned that increasing the volume of their voices was not necessarily abusive. Group provided the interactive process needed for practising acceptable interactive social skills.

What have you found helpful about being a member of a group?

- "We are all pioneers that are part of the first group for male sexual abuse survivors in this area."
- "Although we each come from different walks of life, there seems to be a common thread between us. That common thread consists of: the need to express our pain, the need to give and receive support, the need to give and receive validation, the need to give and receive love, the need to be real, the need to share, the

need for unconditional acceptance, and a need to find and express our voices."

- "Inside these four walls I can express anything about any issue, but it is different outside these four walls."
- "You just can't imagine what this group means to me."
- "What I like about the group is that ownership of the group belongs to the group. We are responsible to ourselves and the group. There needs to be a facilitator, but we are all equals."
- "The sharing of experiences, aspirations and goals."
- "My level of awareness increased as a result of seeing and hearing the separate paths used by others in recovery."
- "The sharing of personal opinions. Learning that the problems you go through are common problems shared by others."
- "Developing a closeness that I have been unable to find in other groups."
- "By other people sharing, I realized I was not alone."
- "I found I could accept what had happened to me."
- "It is helpful to have a confidential, secure, safe and stable place to go."

Talking about vulnerabilities is not considered a "manly act" by a lot of our society. Survivors need to look at how their views on masculinity will effect their growth. They look at the differences between the average man and the average healthy man.

Stage #4: Defining Healthy Masculinity

The meaning of masculinity and self-respect

How do group members view healthy masculinity? What are these men longing for, and how will life be different when they transform and become the people they want to be? What will be their new "meaning" of masculinity?

Defining healthy masculinity

Men from group worked hard at defining masculinity in a way that promotes good mental health. A healthy definition of masculinity includes: men are human beings with insight who are not afraid to look at themselves. Such men know who they are and where they are going. They are not afraid to let others know their feelings. They are respectful, understanding, and kind. They relate well with other men intimately and are content with their maleness. Such men have an understanding of the positive experience of sexuality and are not threatened by women. They understand that to love and be loved are gifts that they can enjoy and nurture.

The most common theme brought up in the group setting is the search for a positive connection with self and others. Their past unhealthy societal views on the "meaning" of masculinity may hinder this search. Without reshaping unhealthy views, many men will struggle with intimate connections with both men and women. Group members have identified how their past views on power, control, and rational thinking have been harmful and restrictive. Many men want to change and are redefining their views. The men from group discuss how their "family of origin" and the culture they live in have shaped their views on masculinity. They often find themselves struggling with a conflict between what they have learned in the past, compared to the direction they wish to take in the future. Before people know where they are going, they must know where they have been.

The first part of this chapter focuses on how group members feel their culture defines masculinity, and what they learned about "being a man." Participants discussed the labels that are placed on men who do not conform to these teachings. They discuss their own definitions of healthy masculinity. The remaining portion of this chapter talks about the importance of friendships and how men can nurture themselves.

What did you learn about "being a man" from the culture you live in?

- "A man is measured by his performance. The better the performance, the better the man."
- "Men must be working at all times and be mechanically inclined."
- "Man must not have insight into himself; his role is to take care of other people."
- "*Real* men are not victims."
- "Men are not allowed to nurture themselves."

- "Men must get over losses quickly and are not allowed to grieve."
- "Men should never confide in other men emotionally."
- "Men must think and not feel; vulnerability is a weakness."
- "*Real* men do not cry, crying is a weakness."
- "Men must be emotionally self-sufficient."
- "Men must be heterosexual and be able to perform sexually on demand."
- "Men are responsible for the female orgasm."
- "Men are seen as abusers, and women are seen as victims. Society views men as inherently problematic."
- "If you are a man, you never let them see you sweat. You have to be tougher than the next guy."
- "Men must anticipate their partner's needs."
- "Men must get married, have children, and change to meet the desires of their wives."
- "Man is a provider and a protector. He must earn a good income."
- "A man must be dominant in his relationships. He must be stronger than women. He must hold and maintain power over women."
- "A man must follow in his father's footsteps."

The above quotes are examples of these men's perceived cultural definitions of masculinity. Many men feel their manhood was measured by their performance; the better the performance, the better the man. The men in-group often described themselves in terms as human-doings rather than as human beings. They do not see themselves for who they are but rather what they do. This is usually based on how they perform for the people around them. Life may seem like a game for these men because they feel as if they are always competing.

Men who have been sexually abused as children find the grieving process to be a difficult, non-traditional-masculine task. Real men are not seen as victims, so victims often do not see themselves as real men. It is difficult for men to show their true feelings when many of these feelings make them appear to be vulnerable and not in control. Grieving and healing are connected to defining masculinity for these men.

Control issues for survivors

Control is a big issue for survivors. Many group members feel they had a sense of control in their lives up until the time of the abuse, and this loss of control cost them much pain and suffering. A method of feeling safe was to be in total control of themselves and everything around them, which of course is impossible. If they were not in control they felt vulnerable and at risk.

They felt they had to be tougher than the next guy. The opposite of being totally controlling is being totally controlled. Some group members became "under-controlling" and left many important decisions in their lives totally in the hands of others. The majority of men requesting counselling feel as if others control them. As people mature in the healing process they tend to think more in terms of influence and feel less need to control or be controlled.

The fact that men struggle with the view that "real men do not need nurturing" makes the recovery process more difficult. Group members feel fragmented when they are limited in expressing their true selves.

Participants were angry that men are stereotypically seen as abusers and women are thought of as victims. This stereotype is especially difficult for men who have been victimized by a woman. They struggle with being a victim, but feel as if they are being portrayed as an abuser. Unfair, one-sided messages are part of the problem, not part of the solution. There are many kind, caring, compassionate men, and there are many assertive, competent women. There are abusive women, just as there are men who are not abusive.

When a traumatic situation happens in a man's life, he is expected to be strong and get over it quickly. Society finds it acceptable for men to grieve the death of a loved one, but only if it is controlled, ends soon, and he shows little weakness. There are many societal myths that hinder men from confiding in other men emotionally. Group members talked about the misconception that men must think and not feel, and how having to be rational all the time is over-rated.

Members thought they had to prove their manhood as a way of being accepted by others. They tried to be somebody they were not as a method of seeking approval.

The more time they spent projecting a false self, the further they detached from their real selves. Is it any wonder that they lost sight of themselves as individuals?

These men want healthy masculinity and wished to be validated by society as good men. They wonder what would happen if they stepped outside of what is considered average in society, and tried a road less travelled. Participants wondered how they would be viewed by their community if they adopted a new way of living.

What "labels" are placed on men who step outside the old views of masculinity?

- "Irresponsible"
- "Fem (feminine)"
- "Faggot, homosexual, gay"
- "Emotionally unstable"
- "Weak, a failure, vulnerable"
- "Queer"
- "Not in control"
- "Flawed, unhealthy"
- "Has many problems"
- "Should be ashamed of himself"

These men explained how hard it was for them to step outside of perceived societal expectations. Although they do not agree with the old definition of manhood, they tried desperately to fit into these outdated expectations. When trying new behaviours that contrasted with a societal view of masculinity, they feared being shamed and labelled as inadequate, queer, or feminine. These men spent the majority of their lives trying to fit into someone else's view of masculinity, without the satisfaction they wanted. They felt flawed when unable to meet those old demands, yet often empty when they did. Life was a difficult and unsatisfying contradiction.

Many men in our society want to step outside of societal norms, redefine masculinity, and become the people they want to be. Participants wanted to feel their entire range of feelings and emotions and choose how they wish to express them. Society will benefit from men who are kind, caring, and compassionate, men who are not controlling or controlled. Group members want to look into themselves, gather insight, and choose a path that is self-directed. These men want to make their own choices, and not fit into the unhealthy patterns that had been passed down from generation to generation. They begin to do this by redefining healthy masculinity.

How do you define "healthy" masculinity?

- "A man can be responsible for himself spiritually, physically, and emotionally."
- "Vulnerability can be our strength and not our weakness."
- "Men can feel good about promoting healthy masculinity."
- "Men have the right to feel and express all their feelings and emotions."
- "A man should be allowed to share all the aspects of his life."
- "A man can have equality with his partner."

- "A man can be dominant and submissive."
- "A man can receive as well as give."
- "A man has the right to nurture himself."
- "A strong man can show vulnerability, empathy, and compassion."

Group members had discussions about how vulnerability can be seen as a strength and should not be seen as a weakness. The group talked about this healthy paradox and how expressing their vulnerability can make them stronger individuals. They felt that a man who talks about his vulnerabilities is stronger than the man who hides his pain for fear of exposing his true self. By getting in touch with and expressing their vulnerabilities to the group, they had an opportunity to become stronger and more in-touch with all the parts of themselves. When they are accepted and validated for who they are, they no longer feel a need to express their false selves. The more validation and acceptance men get in-group, the more likely they will express themselves outside of the group.

Discussing intimacy with men can be a sensitive topic. Intimacy is often confused with sex, and survivors have many fears connected to the word "intimate." Men can be intimate with each other without any thoughts of sex. Intimacy is being "real" with another person and being able to share vulnerable details about their lives. It can be categorized as simply, a warm friendship. This includes interacting with each other in a more genuine, sincere fashion, not only on the football field, but also in the field of life.

It is important for men to have emotional connections outside their marital relationships. Partners can feel overwhelmed when they become the only emotional caregiver for a survivor. If men reach out and support each other, they can have a better chance of achieving needed support, without overloading their partners. Building healthy friendships can be a key factor in an enriched life.

What is a good friend?

- "Somebody you can confide in."
- "Somebody who cares about you."
- "Somebody you do not have to perform for."
- "Somebody who is honest and can tell you the truth."
- "Somebody who shows compassion."
- "Somebody who will let me trust them a little bit at a time."
- "Somebody who will accept me as I am."

It is important for men to be aware if they are lacking healthy connections that could enhance their lives. When men discuss the qualities of a good friendship, they give themselves the framework to evaluate their present interactions with both men and women. Group discussion helped these men to feel more confident when making positive changes in their friendships, without threatening their masculinity.

In examining their relationships, group members were asked to consider: What are the impacts of not having positive intimate connections? How does an unhealthy relationship affect your quality of life? What are the risks involved in making positive change? What fears will you have to face if you want to make some changes? Can you benefit from a change?

Recovering from childhood sexual abuse is a very strenuous challenge, and it is important for people to treat themselves well throughout the process. Part of healing encompasses the transformation from existing to living and learning to put joy into the journey. Members talked about an unwillingness to accept joy until they reached certain recovery goals, thinking their focus should be entirely on change, twenty-four hours a day.

How do I treat myself well?

- "I like to enjoy nature and walk in the bush."
- "Sleep well, paint, draw, and do some writing."
- "Buy some seafood and relax by myself."
- "Listening to music, work in my garden, reading, and spending time with myself."
- "I like to exercise, go canoeing and swimming."
- "I like to eat out."
- "Connect with friends."
- "By getting in touch with my creative side."
- "In the summer, when I increase my exercise, I feel better. There seems to be a connection between my physical and mental health. The better I feel physically, the better I feel mentally."

When the men reviewed the various ways they treat themselves well, they were surprised that none of their activities included performance as a central theme. They questioned why they devoted so little or no time to these healthy activities that make them feel good. Since their worth was mostly based on their performance, self-nurturing was apparently an option only when other areas of their lives were taken care of. The men pointed out that unless they scheduled free time for themselves, they would probably never get any. They all made a commitment with each other to think about themselves when balancing their time.

As men from group made positive changes towards expressing healthy masculinity it was not uncommon for them to feel sad about the stereotyping culture they live in. They felt that expressing their feelings and emotions was rarely rewarded by the society outside the counselling room. They talked about the difficulties of trying to find other men who were willing to express themselves openly.

All group members agreed that their past views of masculinity had hurt them in their pursuit for contentment. They've talked in-group about the struggles they encountered when trying to live up to some of society's views on manhood. This is not just a difficult transition for male survivors; it is also a challenging time for all men. Society is changing very quickly, and many men feel lost in the shuffle. There are many contrasting views on male and female roles in our society. The men from group are challenging rigid views of masculinity and redefining paths that they feel will lead them to healthy masculinity.

What is self-respect?

This above all: to thine own self be true,
and it must follow, as the night the day,
Thou canst not then be false to any man.

— WILLIAM SHAKESPEARE

Self-respect is loving, accepting, and honouring yourself. A counsellor or group leader cannot give self-respect to a man, although he has an important role, much like a coach. Someone else cannot give it to you. You must earn it. Earning self-respect is hard work. Self-respect is different from self-esteem, from pride, from confidence, from discipline, although these may seem the outward representations. Many sexually abused men are considerate and respectful of others, some too much so. They often do not respect themselves as their sexual boundaries were not respected when they were children. Self-respect gives men back to themselves.

Self-respect means active listening to your feelings and your body.

The men in-group acknowledged that the transition from what they had learned about being a man to their present redefinition of masculinity was not a simple task. As men travel through the various stages of recovery, they often recognize that their views change in a way that helps them feel more respect for themselves.

What helps men on the journey to self-respect?

Men want to transform from judging themselves on their performance, to respecting who they are as a person. They want to value themselves for who they are, not just what they do. They do not need to excel at maximum performance in order to be accepted. I was struck when participants said that men could not only give love and support but receive as well. You need to respect yourself to truly accept love.

Most men, survivors and non-victims alike, struggle to find and respect a healthy masculinity. Our society is going through rapid changes, and many men are reshaping how they view their manhood. What makes the process more challenging for men who were sexually victimized is that they often never felt like "real" men. They try desperately to be like everyone else, trying to fit into the "old" views. They had drawn their own conclusions of what kind of man they want to become. Much effort has gone into stereotyping the average man; much less effort has gone into understanding the meaning of masculinity, the healthy man who respects himself and others.

Self-respect is about moving away from the blame or shame games and learning the skills needed to live as a healthy man. Often in-group, men learn to act toward others in accord with developed personal standards of fairness, rather than reacting or retaliating for past actions.

Why is group work effective in self-respect issues?

Men often operate from the outside-in rather than the inside-out, searching for happiness externally instead of internally. They may have "other-esteem" instead of self-esteem. Their esteem is based on how others see them, rather than how they view themselves. It is often hard for them to respect others when they do not respect themselves.

Group provides a fail-safe environment with men with similar backgrounds, who can reflect the man's experience and provide validation and understanding. Men often feel that it is too risky to experiment with self-respect with family or a lover. The group is non-sexual and provides a "safe container" to practice self-respect. Rules are explicitly stated to emphasize safety aspects. The group process also slows down men's processing of their experiences so that they can deal with negative past events and move on. Thus, it is important that the group not move too fast or quicker than the self-respect development of the members allows.

Exercises for building your self-respect:

1. Making choices in difficult times
2. Breaking bad habits
3. Building good habits
4. Setting goals and achieving them
5. Standing up for your beliefs
6. Setting and maintaining your limits and boundaries

7. Completing commitments you make.

8. Standing/sitting up straight, looking people in the eyes

9. Identify and confront abusive or unhealthy relationships, changing what can be changed, moving on when things stay abusive

10. Asking for what you want without apology or complaint

11. Responding 'yes" or "no" without excusing or apologizing

12. Making a list of your positive qualities

Some thoughts on self-respect:

- "Self-respect frees you from the expectations of others, giving us back to ourselves."
- "When we respect others, we give them gifts. With self-respect, we give a gift to ourselves."
- "Not respecting yourself is like slowly committing suicide."
- "Self-respect is something you earn yourself, not something others give you, so no one can take it away from you, without your permission."
- "Self-respect is being able to identify and value your own strengths."
- "Self-respect is self-esteem in action."

Exploring healthy masculinity helps pave the way to the next stage of recovery. The next stage of recovery provides the energy needed to keep the momentum going.

Stage #5: Anger

Anger is a pivotal part of the healing process. When survivors reach this point, they often feel alive and powerful, possibly for the first time in their lives. Anger can be very challenging, and victims are often sceptical when expressing the feelings underlying their anger. They may be afraid to experience and express these feelings for fear they will lose control or become vulnerable. On the other hand, they fear if they do not express these feelings they will not feel whole. Many survivors have a build-up of anger inside themselves, fearing that if tapped into, they may be lost in rage forever.

Many men enter individual counselling with the hope of learning new skills to eliminate anger. They seemed surprised when told this in not just unobtainable but perhaps an undesirable goal. Anger is a natural, necessary feeling that is essential to their healing process.

Anger is an emotion, nothing more, nothing less. It can be right, wrong, or even illogical at times. How people choose to respond to their anger, their *behaviour*, determines if it is healthy or unhealthy. Anger is often confused with behaviour, and it is important to separate the two. We do not need total control over which feelings we experience, but we do need to exercise a choice on how they respond to these feelings. How we react determines the outcome. Anger is like gasoline. If you use it wisely it can give you fuel for your journey; if you do not use it wisely, it will blow up in your face.

Anger is a secondary feeling that follows other feelings. Imagine yourself driving down the highway in your car, and suddenly somebody cuts you off, causing you to slam on your brakes and swerve to the side of the road. You may think you would get immediately angry with the driver in the other car. Anger is probably not the first thing you felt. Perhaps you would feel scared for your life or powerless over the situation. Before your anger surfaces, you may have felt shock. Anger follows other feelings.

Anger is energy that gives you an opportunity to resolve conflict. It lets you know something does not seem right in your life. Perhaps your rights have been violated and your anger gives you the energy needed to take assertive action to regain self-respect. Maybe you are giving more than you are comfortable giving, and you need to get angry as a way of resetting limits with others. Anger gives you the energy to fuel positive change.

When children are not exposed to healthy role-modelling of anger, they develop unhealthy ways of coping with their own anger. The comments which follow tend to portray parents who were overly aggressive or overly passive. There was not a healthy, assertive balance in between. Children learn from what they see.

What did you learn about anger as a child?

- "If someone got angry, I got the shit kicked out of me."
- "There is no positive way out if someone gets angry. Anger is not productive."

- "You can get what you want through aggression."
- "I learned to never express it."
- "Kids are to be seen and not heard."
- "I could never raise my voice. We had to keep our feelings to ourselves."
- "The only way to be heard was to be angry."
- "The man of the house has the last word. He gets to maintain family dominance."
- "There is always a winner and a loser with anger. If you are less dominant, then you are the loser."
- "Anger hurts. It includes blaming others, being judgmental, and critical. It is a way to gain control over another person."
- "Anger is uncontrollable. It is a wasted destructive emotion."
- "Anger gave them the power to control me verbally, physically, emotionally, and sexually."

Responding to an unhealthy environment depends largely on the personality of individual and the history of the abuse. Some people are more resilient, while others developed fears and anxieties such as: nightmares, bed wetting, fear of strangers, fear of personal safety, and the fear of losing or being abandoned by the abusive person. Most men had a strong attachment between them and the person that hurt them. They feared losing that bond, especially if they had no support outside of the family home.

The dance that gets played out in an unhealthy environment can be confusing. Some men had a tendency to model the behaviour of others and became aggressive in social settings. Their self-concept was affected and they may have viewed themselves as incompetent or limited, thus they didn't take part in activities that could have enriched their lives.

As adolescents, some members gravitated towards high-risk peer groups that focused on anti-social values, causing them to become more defiant and more aggressive. When trying to soothe the feelings of unworthiness, they had a higher risk of substance and alcohol abuse.

Group members found that feelings like fear, abandonment, and grief had often been disguised or substituted with displays of anger. As children, it was far more acceptable for them to display anger than vulnerability. As adults, they recognized this as a learned response. Anything learned can be unlearned, and people can develop new skills.

How did you respond to anger in the past?

- "I would yell and scream."
- "Physically fight with my brothers and sisters, and break things."
- "By getting revenge. Silence meant gaining energy for the next fight."
- "Through addictions such as sex, alcohol, drugs, shopping, and gambling."
- "I would kill animals."
- "By attention seeking and being violent."
- "Silence, stuffing it, starvation, self-abuse, and depression."
- "I would suppress my feelings by overeating."
- "By pretending the situation did not happen."
- "Through self-criticism and shame."

- "I would assume the blame for situations unjustifiably."
- "By not identifying with my true feelings."

It was challenging for these men to unlearn negative information received as children, as they attempted to learn new skills. Due to past experiences in childhood, many men viewed anger as a destructive, useless feeling. Whenever they thought of anger, they thought of somebody getting hurt.

Participants said they had limited memories regarding a healthy expression of anger. They rarely saw others respond to anger in an assertive fashion that brought positive results for everyone concerned. Many men were afraid of their anger fearing their behaviour would resemble their family's responses from the past. Since they viewed anger as being destructive, they chose to mask these feelings and spent most of their lives trying to avoid anger completely.

What fears hinder you from expressing anger?

- "I am scared of the unknown, not knowing what will happen next?"
- "I am afraid of rejection. Will that person accept me?"
- "Fear of abandonment. If I get mad will they leave me?"
- "Fears of losing control. I do not like myself when I lose control."

- "I am frightened that I might hurt someone's feelings. I try to maintain calmness for everybody."
- "Fears of being vulnerable."
- "Fear that others will think it was my fault."
- "I was scared I would kill my abuser."

The men talked about being afraid of anger and viewed anger as a major obstacle in finding their voice. They feared being out of control when thinking about any anger or rage connected to the abuse. Participants questioned what would happen if these feelings were unleashed, wondering if it would take over their lives completely. Talking about their fears automatically reduced the strong hold these thoughts had on them.

Identifying triggers was the next topic of discussion. Some men found they responded to the victimization of others with greater intensity than they did their own. They often told their own stories with little or no feelings, speaking in a soft, inward, monotone voice, as if they were minimizing their own pain. When they began listening and talking about the abuse others had experienced, their voices took on a new shape. The volume increased and their bodies reacted differently. By identifying with the anger connected to other people's stories, they gained insight into their own stored-up reservoir of anger.

Thoughts of revenge would trigger intense anger and rage. They learned that these feelings were also very normal and could help them understand their anger. Fantasies that include revengeful thoughts are a healthy tool for expressing anger, as long as they do not act out on those thoughts. Unfortunately, fantasies can have the potential to make inappropriate action more likely if not regulated in a healthy fashion. They talked about the fantasy of physically hurting the abuser, while some men considered murder. Discussing these fantasies gave them an opportunity to identify with their anger and release it in a non-violent fashion within the group setting. Participants recognized that violence would only satisfy a short-term desire, but in the long run, a jail sentence would cause them more problems than it was worth. Sometimes the best revenge can be living well.

Some members struggled with their anger towards the abuser because they felt personally responsible for the abuse. The men in-group talked about the guilt and shame they carried when their bodies responded normally and naturally to touch; especially if they became aroused sometime throughout the abusive situation. These pleasurable sensations were more difficult to deal with than the hurtful ones. They were confused and embarrassed with how their bodies responded. They took this confusion and misdirected their anger towards themselves, feeling that since there was some physical sensation they must have been partially responsible. This false belief created a barrier or obstacle for them when identifying their anger towards the abuser. Any element of physical pleasure does not diminish the destructiveness of childhood sexual abuse. The men learned to clarify their anger and place the blame directly where it belonged, with the abuser.

What happens when you suppress your anger?

- "I become a doormat and let people step on me."
- "There is an increase in stress, anxiety, and depression."
- "There would be a greater need for medication."
- "You do not develop the skills needed to resolve other problems in life."
- "I would become a people-pleaser."
- "I would not maintain my own self-respect and others would not respect me."

Group members talked about developing skills over the years to suppress their anger, without the desired results they had hoped to achieve. Each time they buried their feelings, it resembled blowing air into a balloon. The more the balloon filled with air the more pressure they felt, often times resulting in unhealthy behaviours when the balloon would burst. They talked about passive-aggressive behavioural patterns. These men attempted to avoid anger completely until they blew up and acted out. After acting-out, the cycle would repeat itself. Some men used legal and illegal addictive substances to delay this cycle.

Suppressing feelings can lead to stress-related illnesses and increase the likelihood of having anxiety and depression. Men complained about tension headaches, upset stomachs, irritable bowel syndrome, and other pains in the body.

When feelings are not expressed in a healthy fashion, they can be manifested into our behaviours. Anger is an emotion that needs to be directed. When not channelled wisely, it gets misdirected towards other less desirable actions, such as violence, and people hurting themselves or others. Statistics show a significant percentage of the prison population convicted of violent crimes were sexually abused as children.

Participants mentioned losing touch with how they feel when anger is not expressed over time. This can lead to losing touch with how others feel. When they gained clarity to how they felt, they developed a greater understanding of how others felt. This led to developing their empathy skills.

Avoiding feelings and emotions can lead to resisting intimate, committed relationships with others. Intimacy requires sensitivity to one's own feelings and to the feelings of others.

People can only be as intimate with another person to the point that they can be intimate with themselves.

What happens when your anger is intensified?

- "My muscles get rigid, there is heaviness in the back of my throat, and I see red."
- "Rage is anger intensified; it is uncontrollable."
- "When I am enraged, my body seems to shake. I get nervous and my speech is loud. I make no sense at times. I lose conscious thought. There is no time to think when I am overloaded with feelings."

- "I lose all my power to resolve issues when I am enraged. Nobody listens to what I am saying because they are too scared of me. I wish I could learn to talk about what is bothering me before rage surfaces."
- "I start to sweat, and the veins in my neck stick out. My kids tell me my face seems to take on a new shape. When I am enraged, nobody else speaks."

Intensified anger or rage is always challenging, both for participants and the people around them. The men mentioned how dangerous it was for them when they did not deal with their anger in the early stages. By not being pro-active they felt their rage turned them into "monsters." When we get angry and lash out, we lose an opportunity to resolve the conflict.

What benefits do you get by inappropriate, angry acting-out?

- "I get power, control, and dominance."
- "There are no delays, I get what I want. It is sometimes easier than talking about it. I get instant results."
- "Quite simply, it works, or at least in the short-term."

The men in-group acknowledged that everything we do is for a reason, and responding to anger in an aggressive fashion can bring short-term results. They could bring an end to arguments when others feared them for their behaviour. It was easier to intimidate someone, compared to being part of a healthy, sometimes uncomfortable process. Unfortunately, inappropriate actions brought them added guilt, distrust and shame.

How to deal with anger effectively

How we respond to anger is a choice and therefore, people are accountable for their actions. These men are not responsible for the abuse they were subjected to as children, but they are responsible and will be held accountable for how they react to their anger as adults. Three popular metaphors used in-group are worth repeating when discussing the topic of anger.

1. We are responsible for our feelings/emotions and others are responsible for theirs.

Members mention how they struggled when trying to take responsibility for their own feelings and emotions. They often found themselves wanting others to be responsible for how they feel, or they put themselves in a position to be held accountable for how others feel.

2. E + R = O. Events in our lives plus our Response equals the Outcome.

This quote comes from a Jack Canfield self-esteem tape. Participants learned that they do not have control over all the events in their lives, but they do have a choice on how they respond. How they choose to respond determines the outcome. Members mentioned they can get caught up in responding to events in the same way, but expected a different outcome. The definition of insanity is to continually respond to events in the same manner and expect a different outcome.

3. I cannot change others; I can only change myself.

This was the group's favourite quote. They often asked each other, "If you do not like your present situation, what are *you* going to do to change it?" or "If you do not change how you respond to the world — then nothing changes and everything will stay on the same path."

A four-point method for dealing with anger seems to be effective. The first step is to acknowledge, we all have various feelings and emotions connected to our anger. Step two is to identify these feelings and give them specific words. Once we know what we are feeling, the third part is to make a rational decision on how much energy we wish to spend on the situation. The final part is to take steps to release any tension. The main focus is to take the anger from within, process it, and bring it outside of the body. When confronted with anger, it is not always worth the effort to take action and that is understandable. Some things in life are just not worth using up our valuable energy. We also do not want to be in denial. If a problem needs to be resolved, then we need to take the appropriate steps towards releasing our anger. Some members released anger verbally, while others developed non-verbal skills. Feelings of resentment are an indication that anger is being suppressed. It is a warning sign to speak up about the problem. Knowing when to express, when not to express, in what fashion to express, and to what degree is appropriate for the moment, is not an easy task.

Anger journal

One of the best ways participants learned more about themselves and how to respond to anger was through the use of anger journals. This is an effective tool for gaining awareness and insight, helping them to be proactive in making change.

These journals document:

- When they got angry. (time and date)
- Why they got angry. What was the situation that sparked their anger?
- What was the intensity level, between one and ten? One was calm and ten was full blown rage.
- What were they physically/emotionally feeling at the time?
- How did they respond to these feelings?
- How would they like to respond differently in future?

Several of the members were not aware of how they responded to various feelings and emotions, and this tool gave them an opportunity to get to know themselves better.

Group members worked hard at getting to know their anger patterns and how their bodies respond to their feelings. The Daniel Jay Sonkin and Michael Durphy book on *Learning to Live without Violence* talks about different levels of intensity and how people respond differently at each level. Men can see these levels on a continuous scale from one (a very low level) to level ten (very high intensity). Level one may be the feeling of ambivalence and ten could be feelings of rage. Participants seemed surprised how often they were unaware of the higher levels of intensity, and how they automatically appeared to suppress the lower levels. By getting to know themselves and putting words to their various levels, they were effectively able to respond to lower levels of anger before they were emotionally overloaded.

When identifying with the different levels, it is important to put words for each feeling within the levels. In levels one, two, and three, men may feel annoyed, bothered, uneasy, jealous, and suspicious. At levels four, five, and six, they may feel nervous, threatened, bitter, disoriented, peeved, and frustrated. At levels seven, eight, nine, and ten, they may feel furious, hateful, fearful, terrified, enraged, and strong. Every person can put their own words to their own unique levels.

Members try to express themselves when things come up, rather than waiting till they blow up. If participants wait until they get to a higher level, they will have less control over their behaviour. When in a full blown rage, it may be too late to think rationally. The men found that as they improved in recognizing and expressing feelings connected to the lower levels of anger, their anger was less likely to escalate to higher levels. One person said he kept so much anger inside that he wasn't surprised it came out in rage. The pressure was so great that it had to come out, one way or another.

The group listed positive ways of overcoming rage.

How do you overcome rage?

- "I express myself when things come up rather than waiting till they blow up."
- "By dealing with reactive anger, I do not have as much anger inside me. The more I deal with residual anger in a safe place, the less likely it is that I will fly into rage."
- "I try to remember that aggression brings more aggression; if I am too passive, I am inviting aggression; and if I practice assertiveness, I will diffuse aggression."
- "I like to become aware of myself and have an understanding where the rage is coming from."
- "When the situation gets too hot, I get away from the situation and leave the area."
- "I try to remember that when in rage my brain is not functioning properly."
- "I concentrate on breathing and slowly relaxing each muscle."
- "I visualize pushing my arms down and out, pushing myself away from the stress, and creating a comfort zone. This technique is similar to my martial arts training."

The men decided to make a list of recommendations to consider when confronted with anger. They felt the more they could educate themselves on healthy choices prior to being upset, the more likely they would be able to respond in a desirable fashion when they did get angry.

What are some positive rules to consider when expressing anger?

- "Consider safety issues."
- "Identify where your anger is coming from."
- "Select a private setting if possible."
- "Think before you sink, take a deep breath."
- "Identify previous anger patterns, and don't repeat past negative choices."
- "Set healthy boundaries."
- "Stay focussed and stick to the issues."
- "Avoid third party arguments; talk directly to the person you are angry with."
- "Use "I" statements and take ownership of your feelings."
- "Be prepared to listen."
- "Practice direct eye contact."
- "If you're angry with someone at work, go through the proper channels."
- "Consider, but do not take ownership of the feelings of others."
- "Face your fears by taking action."
- "Don't criticize."
- "Talk about it with a friend."
- "Take some time to think about it."
- "I like to exercise, go for walks and ride a bike. I also hit pillows, yell, scream, swim, and walk in the woods."
- "Reading, music, and singing can be helpful."

Members stressed the importance of finding both verbal and nonverbal ways of releasing anger. It was essential to direct the anger from within the body to outside of themselves. Some people chose nonverbal forms of expression such as, artwork, dance, writing in a journal, meditation, and walking in nature.

Safety is always the number one concern. Although no setting may feel comfortable, they tried to ensure that they were physically, emotionally, and sexually safe. They would look for an environment that would give them the most amounts of comfort and security possible. If the situation were too dangerous, they would think of other options.

The men from group recognized that they held their breath when they got angry. Conscious breathing helped some of them release tension and lower the level of anxiety. They completed an exercise that illustrated this point. Each of them took their heart rate then inhaled deeply through their noses as they counted to six. While exhaling through their mouths, they counted to seven. This pattern was repeated five times. After completing a series of breaths, they measured their heart rate again and found it was lower and they felt more at ease.

Disagreements with others were often experienced as a win/lose situation. They tried to change this perspective to one where it could become a win/win situation.

They learned that there is no such thing as universal fairness. People have various points of view on a wide variety of topics, and they define fairness based on their own previous experiences. Sometimes it was necessary to agree to disagree and respect each other's right to have an individual opinion.

Anger expressed inappropriately can be very dangerous, and we need to acknowledge this. Some men have stated that others know how to push their "buttons," and as a result, the other person must be responsible for their actions. As men learn to manage their anger, they gain greater control over their own "buttons," and are less likely to blame others for their behaviour. Participants learned that they have choices in how they respond to their thoughts and feelings. Prisons and psychiatric hospitals are full of people who struggle with unresolved anger issues. Many people in prisons have turned their anger outwards, and many people in psychiatric hospitals have turned it inwards.

Many men found it liberating when they felt justifiable anger towards their abuser. They found they were unfairly angry with themselves, when in reality it was the abuser at fault. By redirecting this misdirected anger, it helped them to reduce internal blame and shame. Victims often have a common bond with the abuser; they both wanted the sexual abuse kept secret at all costs. Participants talk about a false image of alliance, and how years later, their loved ones seem suspicious when the victim seemed full of rage, and wanted nothing to do with the perpetrator. Anger often gave these men the energy and motivation needed to separate themselves from unhealthy relationships with their abusers. Fellow group members helped each other stand up against the abuse by putting the blame exactly where it belonged: with the abuser.

Perhaps the group's greatest challenge was to help each other process their feelings. When this topic was discussed, you could see men virtually cringing in their chairs. This was very understandable, most men want to recover from a purely intellectual perspective and think their way through recovery. Survivors often fight their innermost feelings or the messages from within. If they do not explore these inner messages, they may never get to the true meaning.

Participants were encouraged to become their own objective observers and be aware of what their bodies were trying to tell them. It takes time to process feelings, and if expressed too quickly they may lose the true meaning behind the feeling. When these men chose to explore the feelings that lie beneath their anger, they developed new ways to contain their behaviours until their feelings were properly processed. Too many people prematurely express anger.

What are the benefits of assertively expressing anger?

- "I will have a greater peace of mind."
- "There would be a decrease in stress, anxiety, and depression."
- "I sleep better, have fewer migraines, and have more energy."
- "My partner is happier with me."
- "I feel better about myself."

- "I become a better role model for my kids."
- "It helps me learn new ways of dealing with other stresses that happen in my life."
- "It helps me to be real with my friends."
- "I will have a stronger immune system and fewer stomach problems."

When the men began to express their anger more effectively, they eliminated some of the negative symptoms that came with suppression or acting-out inappropriately. When men stood up for themselves and found a respectful assertive voice, they developed skills that helped them feel empowered and proud. It gave them a sense of self-worth and self-respect.

Some positive rules to consider when expressing anger with your children

- "Kids need unconditional love and acceptance. You can consequence the behaviour, but still show love to the child."
- "Take responsibility for your anger; do not take it out on the kids. Your anger is yours to own."
- "You need to do your own anger work when upset with the kids."
- "Separate residual anger from reactive anger."
- "Allow your kids to speak before "flying off the handle."
- "Remember that your kids will probably grow up and adopt your style of dealing with anger."

Breaking the negative cycle of anger passed down from generation to generation can be empowering. When men traced back their family patterns of dealing with anger, they found a long history of inappropriate expression. These patterns ranged from being overly aggressive to overly passive. The thought of breaking this cycle and passing on positive skills that would enhance their children's lives gave them the motivation to strive for new growth. By improving skills with their own anger patterns they were helping to shape healthier relationship skills for their children.

Group members determined how their own individual childhoods had influenced their adult behaviour. They gained an understanding of themselves and how they related to their children. These men were concerned about the needs of their children, and several men had educated themselves by getting books from the library, individual counselling, contacting local organizations that specialize in the needs of children, and joining a support group.

Is change possible when it comes to expressing anger? Can new behaviours be learned? Absolutely. With effort, people can definitely change how they respond to their anger. Anything learned can be unlearned, and we all have the ability to learn newer, healthier ways of releasing anger. Anger can become a healthy, productive feeling.

Stage #6: Depression

Depression is mainly defined by the culture we live in. Group members look not only at depression, but how society defines it. The current definition is one-dimensional and approached mostly from a biological perspective, which is primarily treated by medication. The medical model seems to have reduced too many problems to a disease perspective. This approach leaves people feeling powerless to participate in their own change. When we reduce the effects of trauma to a disease model, we tend to advocate drugs too heavily. Men who are depressed due to being sexually abused do not have a disease; they have a very large trauma that needs to be worked through. Sexual abuse and dysfunctional environments cause interruptions in development. There is no pill that "re-parents" the child. There is no drug that processes unresolved feelings and emotions. We do injustices to people by only looking at the medical model, and treating most depressions chemically.

Depression comes from a number of places and can be treated in several different ways. If people are told they have a lifetime illness, we take away hope. If we take away hope, we are enhancing depression. By not looking at all possibilities, many men will be vulnerable to the medical model and possibly a lifetime of unnecessary medication.

This chapter defines depression and symptoms that accompany this stage. Participants discuss the origin of depression, combined with the healthiness and unhealthiness of this important stage of recovery. How do people deal with this stage, and what role does medication play in the process?

Men in group explained they had suppressed many feelings and emotions. They feel as if they are taking the lid off of something that has been concealed and buried for a long time. The natural by-product of resurfacing these feelings and emotions is depression.

Depression is a natural and expected stage of sexual abuse recovery. It can be the most challenging stage, but it may result in the greatest amount of growth, which can pave a path to something more desirable. Group members talk about depression as a "conscious rising" phase filled with insight and awareness.

When men enter counselling and support groups, they are engaging in a process of intense growth. For this new growth to happen, they often give up portions of their "old-self." Behaviours that worked for them as children hinder their quality of life as an adult. Patterns that were once useful become outdated and counter productive. Old patterns were not always healthy, but they were familiar, and a natural reaction to giving up old ways of living is depression. Depression helps people to recognize parts of their lives that need adjustment; therefore there must be a healthy component to this process. Giving up old ways of thinking can also produce hope and joy for the future. Some members recognized that clinging to old habits can prolong depression.

Participants looked at the various symptoms that made them aware they were depressed.

What are some common symptoms of your depression?

- "I stop looking at the good things in my life and can only see the bad."
- "I get lost in my emotions and do not realize that feelings are neither right, wrong, nor even logical at times. When feeling bad about myself, I tend to believe my vulnerable feelings, and they convince me I am a bad person."
- "I eat a lot more than I usually do and stuff my feelings."
- "I do not eat as much as I usually do. I just don't care."
- "My mood swings are more often, and for no reason."
- "My sexual desires tend to decrease, reaching out and connecting with somebody seems impossible. I do not feel loveable and don't feel like loving others."
- "By withdrawing from my family and friends, I isolate myself."
- "I can never get enough sleep. I sleep all the time."
- "I never seem to get any sleep."
- "When I am approaching depression or in it, my negative thoughts are intensified. I feel powerless toward positive change. There is a big dark cloud that hovers over me."
- "Memories come up that I thought were no longer an issue with me."
- "I do not think suicide is an option for me, but during depression, I question my quality of life. I feel like life is not worth living, and death seems attractive. I just want to die and pray for God to take me in my sleep."

- "I get lost in my head and find it difficult to stay grounded. Concentrating and making decisions seem overwhelming. I get too wrapped up in self-pity."
- "Activities I once enjoyed become a chore instead of pleasure. Being an active participant in life becomes too scary. I thought people could see me for who I am: an incompetent, disoriented individual. They would see me as a "mental case.""
- "I often put labels on myself. When something negative happens, I tell myself I am a loser. I improperly think that any negative event must happen because I am inadequate. I pick out something bad and focus entirely on it and do not see other parts of my life."

Some survivors talk of unexplainable physical problems such as: stomach aches, persistent headaches, digestive problems, irritable bowels, and pains in other areas of their bodies. They now try and listen to what their bodies are trying to tell them and then take the appropriate action.

If you or somebody you know is experiencing a number of the symptoms mentioned, find appropriate help and remember that depression is a natural, normal response in sexual abuse recovery. Traveling through depression is an important, necessary step towards achieving mental health. Seeking support is a sign of courage and strength. If you are depressed, consider talking to a counsellor and explore the various options available to you.

Where does depression come from?

- "It started with living in a shame-based family. My thoughts create my pain. My negative view of myself does not help me any. Ever since I can remember, my parents made me feel like I was flawed."

- "My childhood upbringing taught me how to be helpless and shame-based. It gave me the coping skills that enhanced depression as an adult."

- "It comes from being sexually abused as a child. It is like I see the world through a foggy lens. I developed a distorted view of the world. Depression brings an awareness of this distortion. Recovery is a reconstruction of my views in an attempt to clear the fog."

- "Dealing with my family and society depresses me. My whole family suffers from depression and so do I."

- "The one thing I know for sure is that sexual abuse is my main concern."

- "Depression comes whenever I try to make a major change in my life that affects my coping skills."

Group members recognized that many of the statements listed are blaming statements, which limit them from taking responsibility for their feelings. Although these facts about the past are true and accurate, they found themselves taking more responsibility for their feelings as the group process evolved.

Many men mention that a portion of their depression originated in their family upbringing. Living in shame-based families contributed to negative views of themselves. One person said that ever since he could remember his parents made him feel like he was flawed. If a parent constantly tells a child that he is bad or flawed, that child grows up into an adult believing he is bad and flawed. Parents need to acknowledge that how they speak to their children will be how their children will speak to themselves as adults.

Research suggests that women are twice as likely to be diagnosed with depression as men, and men are twice as likely to abuse alcohol. It may be that just as many men may suffer from depression as women, but cope with it differently. Why are so many men suffering from addictions? Why are so many men in prison? Why do so many men commit violent crimes? Why is there so much risk-taking, self-destructive behaviour in men? The men in group felt that in our society it is more acceptable for men to stay addicted and hide behind substances than to talk about the sexual abuse they were subjected to as children.

Men who join a support group and explore the feelings and emotions underlying their pain are far more likely to overcome depression compared to men who frequent the local pub. Depression can be more prevalent at certain times of the year.

Does depression follow a pattern?

- "I feel good in the summer and bad in the winter. Spring feels good when I see new life in nature. I relate to the new growth, and try to envision myself as a growing plant, with a new beginning and new hope."

- "My depression was seasonal. I would always get depressed in the winter. There was nothing to do, but stay indoors."
- "I get depressed every summer. I do not like my body. Everyone else exposes their bodies in the summer."
- "Depression usually comes every Christmas. Holidays are very hard on me."
- "I get depressed when watching TV programs that talk about sexual abuse."

Many people find winter to be a dark, dreary time. In fact, some men did not participate in support groups throughout the summer. When fall sets in and winter approaches there seemed to be a noticeable increase in the men requesting services.

Members talked about depression resurfacing during holidays and the Christmas season. A large number also experienced some form of stress and anxiety once the holiday or event had passed. These feelings of despair were caused by: increased stress and fatigue, unrealistic expectations of themselves and others, the increased demand for materialism, shopping, parties, and getting together with people they would rather not spend time with. Old, out-dated coping skills often resurfaced during these difficult times. They were relieved when they found new ways to cope as a way of minimizing or eliminating holiday depression.

The group talked about the unhealthiness of depression and how it had a debilitating effect on their daily life. Some members got stuck in depression and found it challenging to find a way through the pain and discomfort. They learned that depression was often a choice and that some people choose to remain in that posture. The safety of isolation may have seemed more appealing then taking risks and reaching out. Other men said they got more attention from others when they were depressed. Some men felt they had no choice in the matter; their depression seemed too overwhelming and uncontrollable. When they got stuck and were not moving towards insight and action, they reached out and spoke to a counsellor.

What are the disadvantages of depression?

- "You can get very sick if you are not careful."
- "It can kill you."
- "Unfortunately, others around you can be affected and hurt."
- "You lose the opportunity to do more enjoyable things in life."
- "You lose the opportunity to enjoy the holidays and special occasions."
- "I feel useless when I am depressed."
- "When I take out my pain on others, I feel bad." "It can take all of your energy away."
- "You can feel suicidal and make actual attempts on your life."
- "It can destroy friendships and marriages."

Depression can be a serious problem, which justifies a reason to be concerned. Remember, it is a sign of strength and not weakness to ask for help. Participants commented that they could get very sick if they were not careful, and it could possibly lead to death. Members stressed strongly to each other that if someone is depressed, get help.

There are many scary aspects of depression. Members stated that the lack of hope seems overwhelming when in the pits of despair. But it was extremely important for them to look at the bright side of depression. It gave them an opportunity to evaluate themselves and make positive choices that would enrich their lives.

What are the advantages of depression?

- "It can be a warning sign."
- "When I get depressed, I realize my life is out of balance."
- "I am healthier as a result of my past depression. I would not have made the changes I made, if it were not for my depression."
- "It helps me to make major life changes."
- "Dealing with depression has made me a stronger person. I used to run and hide from my pain. I used to seek incarceration in jail. Before, it helped me get away from the rest of the world, where I did not feel safe. People could hurt me emotionally if I was on the outside. It worked for me at the time, but it does not work for me now."
- "Depression can be my friend."
- "It forced me to reach out to others for help. I now have a larger support team."

- "It helps me to make positive changes in my life."
- "Depression is a natural part of the grieving process."
- "It is a sign that something is not right in my life and depression has helped me to balance out my feelings and emotions. I used to eat my feelings away."

Talking about the healthiness of depression may seem uncharacteristic to some people. Depression serves a purpose. The body is trying to bring awareness to unfinished business. These men were in situations where their life seemed out of control, and depression was simply defined as lack of hope. By looking at depression as an opportunity for positive change, there began to be light at the end of the tunnel. One of the biggest advantages mentioned was insight.

Insight comes from having an objective view of your true self. If a person's life is out of balance, they may not like what they see. If they do not like what they see, they may get depressed. If they work through that depression and choose a different way of life, they may be ultimately happier.

One group member questioned the healthiness of depression. He acknowledged that his depression gave him insight and awareness, and that when he spent time alone, he often got depressed. He asked the group an important question: if depression brings him insight, should he seek time alone to be depressed? The answer to this question was not easy for the group to define, and like many answers, it was both "yes" and "no." Dealing with depression in a healthy way can be a call to go inwards, giving him a deeper understanding of himself and the world around him. It can be an indication that something was not working in his life, and he may benefit from a change. This man talked about the loneliness of spending time alone, while others expressed the enjoyment of having time for themselves and saw it as a time for reflection. Being alone does not necessarily resemble depression. The group stressed how important it was for him to learn to like himself and enjoy his own company, and that would bring him to a place of feeling comfortable when alone. He then could seek time alone for insight and awareness and not necessarily loneliness and depression.

Members mentioned that being aware of their old patterns of behaviour and triggers helped them to identify potential difficulties. It was easier for them to plan for the future when feeling well than it was to wait until they were overwhelmed by feelings of sadness and despair. By planning ahead, they found they could either minimize or eliminate a deep depression.

One member explained that depression was a sign that something was not right in his life, and facing depression had helped him to balance out his feelings and emotions. He said he used to "eat his feelings away," and now depression gives him the awareness that something is wrong. He talked about overeating and how this was a problem for him. When he learned that part of his growth was to learn that he was stuffing his feelings and emotions as a way of avoiding unresolved issues in his life, he decided to talk about his feelings. This man is happy with his new skills, but reflects how hard it was to give up those cherry pies. Finding new skills meant taking risks and walking into something that was not familiar to him.

Another member said depression had made him a stronger person, and how he used to run and hide from his pain. He would seek incarceration in jail because it helped him get away from the rest of the world where he did not feel safe. People could hurt him emotionally if he was on the outside. It worked for him at the time, but it does not work for him now. This isolation was a coping skill that served a purpose until he realized it was robbing him of the opportunity to interact positively with others, which was restricting him from the opportunity to love and be loved. He found that working through his anger and dealing with depression helped him plan for a better future.

One man said he lived a life of pleasing others, and how as a child, he never felt loved unconditionally. He felt his worth was determined by how he performed, and the evaluation of this worth was based on his ability to please others. This pattern carried on into adulthood. He spoke energetically and with passion about the struggles he encountered when trying to give up that part of his old self. He had difficultly identifying his needs and learned he was a valuable human being for who he was, and not just what he did. The group reminded him that he is a human being, not a human doing, and how those out-dated, unhealthy coping skills served a useful purpose for many years. Those skills worked and were useful in his past environment, but now they represent a greater cost than benefit. This man was depressed when he confronted his old coping skills, but by working through them, he became empowered and found better ways to cope.

Members cautioned each other to be aware when old coping skills would resurface. They recognized that drinking alcohol caused their depression to escalate. When they began to get depressed they tried to spend time with people who were safe and supportive. Loneliness was an indicator to reach out and be with others. Some men found it comforting to help others. Some men found themselves trying to "over-please" others at their own expense, so they learned to sit back, take a deep breath, and re-evaluate the situation.

How do people deal with depression? What do they do that is helpful when trying to find their way out of the fog? Even though most research seems to indicate that some combination of medication and counselling is the most therapeutic approach, most group members said they had negative experiences with what they felt was the over prescribed use of medication. Any discussion on medication triggered anger amongst group members.

What role does medication have with depression?

- "I have to stay away from chemicals and concentrate on changing my lifestyle."
- "I took positive steps in changing my life. Antidepressants did not work for me."
- "Society pushes medication on you. They want short-term results. They do not look at long term

results of alternative approaches. Group has been far better for me than any drug."

- "I understand that doctors and psychiatrists do not have time to listen to you. It is easier to give me drugs than listen to me."

- "I feel much better when I control my own thoughts and feelings. I would rather work through my problems than mask them with drugs."

- "Antidepressant medication made me feel better at times, but the side effects just were not worth it. I felt as if I did not own my feelings and emotions. They were controlled more by the drugs than they were by me. I like owning my feelings, good or bad."

- "You can get addicted to the medication doctors prescribe, and then you will have more problems."

- "Doctors are scared of trying alternative treatments."

- "Drugs are a short-term solution and do not get to the root of the problem."

- "When my doctor talks about chemical imbalances, I get confused. My depression comes from several areas. The sexual abuse from the past is environmental. I have a negative outlook, which is psychological, and perhaps I have a chemical imbalance, which is biological. I cannot tell you what my neurotransmitters or the chemicals in my brain are doing right now, but I do know that the more I get help for the sexual abuse the better I feel."

Depression is often defined by the medical community as an imbalance of chemical messengers or neurotransmitters in the brain. This is a biological, biochemical imbalance that is viewed as a chemical imbalance and often treated with antidepressants.

I do not take a black and white position on the use of medications, but the non-pharmaceutical treatment for depression needs to be explored. It can be irresponsible to give people medication without first exploring alternative treatments. Addressing problems is far more effective in the long run than finding short-term solutions for symptoms. Members felt that society pushed medication on them and that doctors and psychiatrists emphasized short-term results. All participants felt support groups had been far better for them than any drug.

Pills can be a very necessary part of mental health when prescribed and monitored by a professional, who is trained in psychopharmacology, and prescribed in conjunction with other non-chemical treatments, such as counselling. An important component of prescribing medication is to develop a plan that will eventually eliminate the use of these prescriptions. Sometimes people are so depressed, they need medication to bring them up to a point where they can work on their issues. There are some people who may need medication over a longer period of time and possibly indefinitely. This is often the case with people suffering from severe mental health disorders.

Many male survivors have been misdiagnosed with a mental disorder when their symptoms from historical abuse resembled the symptoms of a biological disorder. Medication can be like putting a fresh paint job on a rusty car. The car will look good for a short period of time, but the problem will resurface. If we treat historical abuse with pharmaceuticals, we may be masking the problem. It then becomes a band aid solution. The group strongly felt that counselling was a preferable approach for them.

Finding appropriate help was a difficult task for these men, especially when they experienced deep feelings of despair and lack of hope. Participants encourage others to keep looking until they find an appropriate counsellor that they are comfortable with. Perhaps family, friends, or others who are knowledgeable on this topic can be of assistance. People can contact local organizations that specialize in sexual abuse recovery. Group members feel the search for an understanding, supportive counsellor is essential. They want this person to be knowledgeable and approachable. Participants wanted to be as comfortable as possible when discussing the many issues and vulnerabilities surrounding their recovery. They recognize that counsellors differ in approaches, beliefs, and philosophies. When possible, interview the counsellor and choose an approach that best works for you. You do not have to stay with the first support person you talk with. The choice is yours.

Members felt the counselling environment facilitates a healthy transition through depression; a place of unconditional acceptance. This "safe place" gave them an opportunity to experience and express feelings that were at the root of their concerns. The counsellor and the support group provided a sense of hope and self empowerment.

These participants learned that a proactive approach to depression was helpful. The first step was to identify the problem. Once they were more aware of the problem, they developed a plan. Participants said that their bodies would let them know when their lives seem out of balance, and they made a commitment to each other to respond appropriately to these signals. Support groups helped guide them throughout the process.

They learned that, at certain times of the year, they were more prone to depressive thoughts. These men tried to keep expectations for the holiday season manageable. They planned in advance and set realistic goals for themselves, being compassionate about what they could and could not achieve. Holidays do not make the feelings connected to the sexual abuse automatically vanish. Each holiday season was different, and these men learned to enjoy them in their own way, at a pace they were comfortable with.

Depression is an opportunity to become aware, and this awareness can facilitate positive change. By being proactive and working through the stage of depression, it can bring people to a healthier place. As people work through the stage of depression, they enter into the next stage of clarifying feelings and emotion.

Stage #7: Clarifying Feelings and Emotions

Clarifying feelings and emotions is part of discarding parts of the "old self" that no longer serve a useful purpose. The self awareness gained by clarifying feelings and emotions pave the way towards letting go and making room for a new, more authentic self to emerge. The more people process their feelings, the further away from depression they travel. This is an insightful stage that helps men come in contact with the hurt inner child they left behind. There is a very wide range of conflicting feelings and emotions that take place throughout the journey. By exploring the feelings connected to the grieving process men are able to bring clarity to their thoughts and feelings.

Forty-five feelings connected to the grieving process

One group session was dedicated to a "feelings and emotions" exercise. Participants talked previously about feelings of anger, hatred, and rage but seemed to struggle with identifying and expressing a wider range of feelings.

A list containing approximately forty-five different feelings was circulated to the group members. This list contained: angry feelings, fear feelings, pleasurable feelings, disorientated feelings, wanting feelings, sad feelings, and unmotivated feelings. The men were asked to think of a stressful situation, look at the feelings list, and come up with a sentence describing each word in relation to how they felt. They had to include the feeling word in the sentence.

Upon viewing the list, group members expressed their insecurities with doing this exercise. One member commented that he had never expressed these feelings in his life and did not know what half of the words meant. Several men questioned their intelligence. What seemed in theory to be a simple exercise was truly a difficult one. These men sensed that this exercise was going to bring them to the roots of their sexual abuse experience. There was no escaping vulnerability and pain in this session. Participants requested an early break to determine how they wanted to proceed. Several members were ambivalent, but they all chose to continue. Talking about these feeling words turned into an intense triggering experience. The exercise was both intellectually challenging and emotionally draining. Participants had a difficult time saying the sentences without truly feeling the words. Some of the most academically educated people found this to be the most challenging of exercises, recognizing that there is a difference between cognitive and emotional intelligence. The energy felt in the room was at an intensity level I never felt before. The men in group worked through their fears and continued.

When choosing a stressful situation to describe, each person chose an experience that included being sexually abused as a child. They were asked to state one sentence that included the feeling word provided. Every sentence below includes the feeling word, which is listed in bold type.

- "I am **angry** that I was not allowed to express my feelings."
- "I get **annoyed** when my feelings and emotions are sparked by triggers."
- "I get **bitter** when others do not act appropriately towards abuse issues."
- "It's **frustrating** how people treated me after I disclosed the abuse. Nobody would help me."
- "I became **furious** when others didn't let me express my anger."
- "I have **hatred** towards the perpetrator for what he has done."
- "I am **peeved** that the perpetrator has left me with so much pain."
- "**Rage** surfaces when I can't resolve my issues, I feel powerless."
- "There seems to be a lot of **fear** of the unknown."
- "When I lose control in relationships, I feel **frightened.**"
- "I am **scared** of what the outcome may be when I speak up against the abuse."
- "I am **anxious** to resolve my past."
- "I get **hysterical** at times and yell, holler, and scream."
- "I get **nervous** and feel that I am losing it when I tell my story."
- "I am **terrified** of what others will think of me."
- "When controlled by others, I feel **threatened.**"
- "When I get put into a situation where I think I am being taken advantage of, I feel **vulnerable.**"
- "I wanted **affection** but got abused instead."

- "I **love** myself for grieving the abuse. The root of the problem was learning to put those thoughts and feelings into words."

- "I am **pleased** that I can do something about the abuse in a natural way. Staying away from medication is good for me."

- "When the police didn't give me the answers I need, I got **confused.**"

- "When I feel out of balance, I get **disoriented.**"

- "I am **suspicious** that the church knew what was happening and chose not to do anything about it."

- "I get **flustered** when society does not do the right thing. The perpetrator gets more help then the victim."

- "I am **sceptical** about the views of the church."

- "When dealing with another person's feelings, I become **ambivalent.**"

- "I am **bothered** when I think that the outcome of my disclosure could be bad."

- "It makes me **uneasy** knowing that my situation will take a long time to resolve."

- "I feel **lonely** when nobody tried to understand. When nobody believed me, I felt life wasn't worth living."

- "When people say "no" to me, I feel **rejected.**"

- "I had a **longing** for positive attention. My needs are important too."

- "I feel **empty** that my mother knew something was wrong and did not do anything about it."

- "When the perpetrator gets more attention than the survivor, I get **jealous.**"

- "When I search and search for answers and nothing comes up, I feel **sad.**"

- "I feel **melancholy** when I'm down in the dumps."
- "I get **weepy** when my voice will not come out."
- "I got **miserable** when I could not get the love I desire."
- "I feel **guilty** because the abuse went on for so long."
- "I felt **remorse** when my aunt was dying, and I did not know how to help her."
- "I feel **lethargic** because the perpetrator has more strength than I do."
- "At times, I feel **lazy** and have no energy to change the situation."
- "It is **exhausting** fighting for my strength."
- "I feel **powerless** when people will not listen to me and there is nothing I can do."
- "I feel **hopeless** when I see no light at the end of the tunnel."
- "I feel **helpless** when I had no control and nobody would help me."

To effectively feel the impact of this exercise, choose an experience in your life that seemed emotionally overwhelming and complete the exercise on your own.

Most of the feelings listed are vulnerable ones, but there are many positive feelings involved in the healing process. Several pleasurable feelings may include: pleased, delightful, high, elated, cheerful, blissful, loving, joy, and affection. There are also many confidence feelings, such as: strong, confident, bold, trusting, sure, energetic, keen, helpful, eager, inspired, and powerful. Some satisfied feelings include: calm, glad, peaceful, satisfied, blissful, and adequate.

What proved to be the most educational component of this exercise was defining each feeling. This method helped everyone to:

- Acknowledge and identify with a wide range of feelings.
- Recognize many conflicting feelings connected to events from the past.
- Provide education to each other when defining the various feelings.
- Learn how to incorporate the use of different feelings into their vocabularies.
- Learn how they substituted anger and aggression with other feelings and emotions.
- Gain another tool to get in touch with how they felt.

As these brave men worked through this exercise, they continued down the grieving process. The most effective way to grieve is by travelling right through the centre of grief. By expressing the feelings and emotions connected to the sexual abuse these men were gaining skills that could help them grieve situations that occur in the present. They walked away from group with a better understanding of themselves. Healing from grief does not mean that they will never hurt again, but they will certainly feel differently about their past. The abusive situation becomes more of an objective experience then a subjective one. As people move further away from the abuse they tend to view the victimization they experienced from the eyes of an objective observer, without the painful feelings and emotions of the subjective experience.

Grieving and letting go

Grieving includes the feelings, emotions, and thoughts connected to a loss in someone's life. Grief is a natural healthy process that does not occur without some pain and discomfort. It is not uncommon for survivors to be misdiagnosed as having some form of mental health disorder, when in reality, they are simply working through unresolved issues from the past. Grieving is not a mental illness, or a disease. It is a perfectly natural and normal part of being human and responding to a traumatic event. This is nature's way of processing pain. Time alone is not a healer, but dealing effectively with time is. Grieving is not linear; it's back and forth and all over the place. It can appear when least expected, triggered by everyday events. Unresolved grief is like a time bomb, and when not expressed in a healthy fashion, it could come out in behaviours, or in the form of illness.

Survivors found it very important to express the various feelings connected to their past experience. When they travelled around the perimeters of grief, they found these issues remained unresolved. These unresolved issues caused them to endure future emotional, psychological, or physical consequences. As children, they did not have the opportunity to feel their feelings and express them with safe and supportive people. The hardest part of grieving was to revisit and re-experience any feelings connected to the loss. Participants talked about the loss of their innocence, the loss of their childhood, and the loss of an opportunity to develop healthy sexuality. They are travelling back in time and working through the discomfort, but passing through that discomfort leads to a place of comfort.

Four steps to effectively releasing grief

1. Be aware of your past, present, and future views of masculinity.
2. Acknowledge and identify the wide range of feelings and emotions you experience.
3. Find your voice and put your thoughts and feelings into words.
4. Develop new coping skills with identifying and getting needs met.

These men found it useful to develop insights into their past, present, and future views of masculinity. This helped them to identify any possible obstacles that hindered their expression of feelings and emotions. They looked at the past to determine what they had learned, the present to determine how they were responding to what they have learned, and the future to practice new ways of expressing themselves. Group members encouraged each other to express grief rather than suppress it. By expressing themselves, they worked through their pain, rather then delaying healthy grieving. Many people delay the process for years, while some avoid it for a lifetime. Participants all agreed that avoidance was no longer an option.

Stage #8: Regrouping

Finding your voice

When discarding parts of the "old self," it can be challenging to connect with the true, more authentic self. Participants said they spent most of their lives trying to be someone they were not. Trying to be the person other people wanted them to be. They spent most of their lives hiding from the pain connected to the sexually abusive experience, thus creating a "false self." Finding their true voice was an empowering process that enhanced feelings of self worth.

Participants discovered that finding their voice and putting their thoughts and feelings into words brought them closer to a positive connection with self. Over the years, they feared putting a voice to their feelings, for fear of hurting themselves or someone else. As they became more comfortable with their voice, they gained strength and confidence. This helped them to overcome personal obstacles that had troubled them for years. The members of the group used their voice as a tool for becoming real and getting closer to their true selves.

Most people struggle with finding their true voice. Participants talked about a lifetime of feeling disconnected from their true selves. Most of them felt split, as if they had several personalities living inside their bodies. They sensed having had two identities. One identity was a true self, which was mostly hidden and not talked about. The second identity was a false self, which they projected to the world around them. This is common for a large portion of our population.

The false self was part of their social self, which they portrayed to people around them. Members talked about how they put their own needs last and pretended to be in control. They needed a false self persona to prove to others that they were "okay." They did not like what happened to them as a child and viewed the abuse as part of their core identity. By attempting to show the world that they were not hurt by the abuse, they distanced themselves from a part of them that still needed to heal. The more they developed skills to hide their true feelings, the more they lost touch with their "true self." The more they became disconnected, the harder it was for them to express a voice representing their true self.

Members were asked to put everyone else's opinions aside and explain how they would like to proceed with their own life. They were stumped, and said how difficult it is to express their own wants and needs. The voice that often led them was something the group referred to as the "negative critic." This is self-talk that influenced them with thoughts of guilt and shame. Most people can identify a person from their past who resembles this negative critic. Parents must be careful with the tone of voice they use on their children, for when their children get older, they will use that same tone of voice on themselves.

Support groups provide a place to bridge the gap between the false self and true self. Fellow members were not interested in anyone pretending to be somebody they were not. They valued being real with each other and themselves. Even though it was challenging, participants practiced having a voice that represented how they honestly felt. This gave them an opportunity to look inward and evaluate what was better for them, the old voice or the new one. Being real felt much better than acting.

Part of being real is having a voice that expresses an individual's wants and needs. Members tried to be confident and assertive when they expressed this voice, but it was not a simple task. Some men found that others were not always happy when they started having a voice of their own. This left them with the struggle of deciding whether to change or return to old ways. There is a difference between the average man and the average healthy man.

When these men first entered counselling, they had many conflicting thoughts going through their minds, and they struggled to distinguish one from another. Some felt like they were jugglers, who were juggling ten balls at the same time, but they could only handle five balls comfortably. Stopping to examine any one ball seemed impossible for fear that all the other balls would come crashing down around them.

It was important to verbalize the pain. By getting their thoughts out into the open, they were better able to sort through them and deal with them. If they kept these thoughts spinning in their minds, it was more difficult to gain any clarity or understanding. The more thoughts they had going on in their minds at one time, the more difficult it was to focus on any one specific issue.

By finding and expressing their true voices to others, these men were helping to clarify their own stories for themselves. These men identified the struggles they have with finding their voice and how they overcame these struggles.

What struggles do you have with finding your voice?

- "My wall of silence keeps me isolated from myself."
- "If I express my true self, I feel shame and embarrassment. By exposing myself, people will see through me and know I am flawed, sick, or crazy."
- I had fears how others would respond to me. I took responsibility for how others felt."
- "I take pride in the fact that I do not hurt others with my anger. When I was younger, I was good at keeping my feelings to myself. When my feelings got too big, I would blow up by punching a brick wall; the pain of hurting myself grounded me; the pain brought me back. I struggle with finding a balance."
- "I feel flawed, and by disclosing the sexual abuse, others will see right through me and know I am flawed. I will feel like I am naked and everybody is looking at me."
- "Disclosing information to an insightful group such as this is far different than disclosing vulnerabilities to the general public."

How do you overcome struggles with finding your voice?

- "By confronting my anger, I slowly realized I could express myself without fear of hurting myself and others."
- "Having confidence in myself and expressing my concerns."
- "By confronting my fears."

- "Awareness is the key word. If I have awareness, I can make changes."
- "I learned to be assertive instead of passive and aggressive."
- "It was very important for me to find a male counsellor who understands male issues."
- "Becoming proactive instead of reactive has been useful. There are many ways in which I can improve my life. I've gained control over my life, instead of being controlled by others."
- "I have become more solution focused with: exercise, counselling, group, and treating myself well. I now have more respect for myself, and I work from the inside-out rather than the outside-in."
- "I pick and choose who I open up to. The ghosts from the past are my responsibility. It is important to recognize that there is a big difference between privacy and denial. I do not deny my problems but I do pick and choose how and whom to resolve them with. Not everyone needs to know my past."
- "Talking to a therapist and joining a support group got me started."
- "I have phoned the crisis line when I felt bad."

It is quite amazing to witness the beauty of an open, honest conversation. Being real is truly magical, and we would all live in a better world if more people chose this method of interacting with each other. By providing a safe and supportive environment, these men had an opportunity to express themselves. Participants often struggled with articulating what their past experiences really meant to them. Understandably, it was very difficult for them to talk openly and honestly about situations that they were confused about. Members said it felt like they had to force the words out from within. The fact that they were even speaking about the past was a tremendous accomplishment. It did not matter how they said what they needed to say. The fact that they were talking about the past was encouraging.

How do you struggle with finding your voice in relationships?

- "I feel like I am naked in the desert when I express my vulnerabilities. When expressing my concerns with another individual, I am setting myself up for rejection if that interest is not returned."

- "I do not know how quickly to open up emotionally and how deep I can go."

- "I am not sure if I can talk about the sexual abuse and the effects it has had on my life. I do not want to scare my partner away."

- "When emotions and feelings surface in a relationship, old wounds open up, and I feel like my growth has back tracked. I question the good things I have done in recovery; I feel like I am starting over."

- "It is easier to push people away than it is to ask them to come closer. Then at least you do not have to fear rejection."

- "When I express my story, I talk with little or no feeling."

- "I was always the giver, and my partner was the taker. When I started taking care of myself, she did not want me anymore."

- "It is hard to find someone who understands, somebody you can trust and talk to."

- "I try to feel positive about my growth, and at the same time, my friends tell me to forget about it, it happened a long time ago. They tell me I do not need counselling. They do not like the changes they see in me, even though I know they are good changes."

- "As I disclose, grieve, and work through my issues, many of my friendships are hindered, challenged, or lost."

These men talked about a desire to have close intimate relationship with others. They longed to be loved, touched, and accepted as a loveable, loving person. At the same time, they recognized they were keeping others at a distance. With one hand, they would reach out, and with the other, they would push away. This would send mixed messages to potential intimate connections. As children, they had been betrayed by someone they loved and trusted; people that they let get close to them. The abuser violated that trust, and they felt betrayed. Participants fear trusting others, assuming past experiences would be recreated in the present. Members explained that some of their greatest fears surfaced when their relationships seem to be going well. They often traced these feelings back to the time of the abuse; a time when they allowed themselves to get close and be vulnerable. Just when they felt everything was good, the abuser would victimize them. They learned that trusting could result in long-term pain. As adults, they still feel this pain, and they are very hesitant to take what seems like a life-threatening risk to be intimate with others.

Unfortunately, many relationships do not stay intact throughout the recovery process. One man mentioned how scared he was to grow as a person. He explained how his interactions with his partner were based on his "old self." If he were to grow, the relationship would be forced to grow as well. Concerned that his wife would not make these adjustments, he talked about staying unhealthy so that his relationship would not be threatened.

How do you overcome struggles to express yourself in relationships?

- "By grieving the past, I ensure that I do not transfer my issues to my relationship in the present."

- "Expressing and getting to know myself in a relationship was a real growth opportunity, not only did I practise relationship skills, I was able to take a look at my past and address any unresolved issues."

- "I had to take a look at the situation of control verses influence. We have an influence in our relationships, but we do not have total control. Remember there are two individuals, and be careful not to take ownership for the other person's feelings."

- "I have learned a lot of things since I last dated. Now I get to apply them, even though it is pretty scary. In the past, I was living in denial; now that I am aware, I feel that dating will be entirely different and unfamiliar."

- "I find I give better when I feel better about myself. The more I get along with myself, the more I get along with my partner."

How people interact in relationships is partially shaped by their past experiences. When participants recognized that they were unrealistically looking for their partners to fill their childhood voids, they tried alternative ways of working through unresolved issues. Partners can be supportive in the growth process, but everyone is responsible for their own healing process. By having this awareness, these men worked at developing a healthier, more balanced approach.

How is society an obstacle in finding your voice?

- "I kept silent to protect myself from societal myths. There is a myth in society that male victims become abusers, and I do not want to be misunderstood in that category. I felt like I would be judged harshly if I talked about being a victim."

- "Sometimes our emotions can be polarized; we show one image to the public but feel different inside. When I am feeling weak, I show the world my strength."

- "Not everyone wants to hear about my painful past."

- "Society allows us to show our anger but resists when we want to show our pain. I am acceptable when angry but viewed as weak when I express my vulnerabilities."

- "There seems to be few healthy people in society."

- "Society cherishes secrecy, silence, and denial. They do not want to believe what is happening in their own back yards."

Group members view the lack of services available to men as a huge indication that our culture does not value them as members of the community. They wondered why there are not more services made available for male victims? If these services are essential for women, are they not essential for men?

How do you overcome societal obstacles when expressing yourself?

- "I realized I am responsible for my feelings and emotions, and the people I interact with are responsible for theirs. I have the right to express myself in a respectful way."
- "By finding safe and supportive people that are willing to listen."
- "I try to be careful on how I label myself. Labels are dangerous whether we use them on ourselves or others."
- "I realize I have an influence on my environment, but I do not have total control. I cannot make society healthy."

People who work at becoming more insightful are often surprised with how unhealthy society as a whole can be. One member said he sometimes felt like a fixed person in a broken world, but that was better than feeling like a broken person in a broken world. As these men changed and moved toward conscious living, they felt like a minority amongst their friends. Many of the men learned to accept that their communities may never be the safe and supportive environments they desired. Group participants learned to have more confidence in themselves and to choose a path that was best for them.

Expressing yourself in a group of people

One man expressed how he never felt like he "fitted in" when interacting with people in a group setting, and how he often felt invisible. He questioned if it was just him, wondering if he would ever feel like he was part of any group. This man asked the group how he could achieve a sense of belonging, and asked what worked for other members.

Group comments:

- "Try to share common interests."
- "Try to be comfortable with yourself and who you are."
- "Accept yourself, feelings and all."
- "Don't try too hard, go with the flow."
- "Pick out positive interaction skills from others and emulate those skills."
- "Try something different, force yourself to interact. Be open-minded and assertive."
- "Be a good listener and ask others for their opinions."
- "Be careful not to over-analyze yourself or others."

Participants talked about their common insecurities when dealing with people in a group setting. For some men, joining a support group provided a place for committing to deeper relationships, a stepping-stone to improved social skills that could be used outside of group. These men got together weekly to discuss their concerns, and learned that their fears were not that unusual. Learning to support one another helped them to develop positive interaction skills.

Stage #9: Spirituality

As people grow and mature through the stages, they get a sense of power within themselves that is also greater than them. Spirituality is such a mysterious and experiential process that it can not be adequately described with words. People describe a sense of knowing their "true self" when referring to the connection within. This connection provides unconditional love and acceptance that replaces feelings of emptiness and loneliness.

Where you are in your spiritual process is exactly where you should be. Survivors can get caught up in comparing their process with others and unfairly make judgements based on their assumptions. Spirituality is an individual, experiential journey that develops over time. It is a process, and as people work through their recovery, their views on spirituality ultimately change and evolve. RYHSR groups are based on the principle we all have the right to establish our own spiritual beliefs. Healing can take place with or without choosing a spiritual path.

Dealing with trust and control issues is a big component of any recovery; however, Spiritual Renovation the most common theme portrayed in group is the longing for a positive connection with self, others, and the environment. Interestingly, group members often view themselves as non-spiritual. Yet, their quest seems very spiritual to me. This quest for connection evolves throughout time and begins with developing a relationship within.

This chapter focuses on spirituality as a stage of recovery, which is necessary for some, but not all. It begins with one man's struggle, followed by the group participants defining spirituality and how they practice their beliefs. Men talk about where they presently see themselves and what they view as a future desire. They discuss how sexual abuse has hindered or strengthened their relationship with a higher power. The chapter ends with Bill giving an overview of his spiritual journey.

Many past relationships for a survivor were filled with trauma and mistrust. When someone is sexually abused at a young age, they learned to fear the world, which includes the people within their community. As children, they were told to trust family but not strangers. When their families betrayed their trust, they learned to trust nobody, including God or any higher power.

When we look at the journey of a boy who was sexually abused at the age of ten, we may gain some insight into his struggles with maintaining a spiritual connection. You may recall Jim's story from earlier in the book. His childhood consisted of living with a family that made him feel flawed whenever his behaviour was not what they wanted. He learned over time that no matter how hard he tried to please his parents, he would never get the love and acceptance he wanted. Jim talked about numerous situations of trying to please them, only to be rejected and ridiculed. This left him feeling unlovable, and he gave up trying to gain their acceptance.

The local minister showed some interest in Jim, and he felt alive. Finally, he found what he was searching for — love, guidance, and safety. He learned to trust that minister and began developing a renewed sense of hope. Jim adored this man and opened himself up to his teachings. After all, this person was a representative of the church and God. How much safer can you get? This minister violated that trust and used his position of power to get close to the boy. Little did Jim know that he was being groomed by a perpetrator. This minister manipulated Jim to the point of sexually abusing him. The abuse went on for six years before Jim realized that he had been tricked, and the minister was just another person who had taken advantage of him.

Jim is a very loveable person, but he felt his childhood experiences proved otherwise. As a child, he did not want to believe he was not loveable, so he adopted the attitude, "I do not need love." The love he experienced had been hurtful, and to protect himself from his pain, he learned to cope by telling himself, "I don't want to be loved." This further progressed to, "I will reject love no matter who gives it to me." He built a wall around himself in an attempt to create safety from the outside world. Jim viewed the local minister as a representative from God, and felt that if God does not care, then nobody would. Jim believed he would be on his own forever without any love or support.

It took several years for Jim to break the cycle of this belief pattern. If spirituality is a relationship with self, others, and nature, you can understand why Jim was hesitant to embrace this concept. His past experiences with relationships did not represent his version of a loving God. He developed a sense that he was flawed and thought the abuse must have been his fault. This was his way of making sense of the victimization. His love relationships were conditional, short-term, and hurtful.

Members questioned how trust and faith are interconnected. How could they not trust other people but yet have faith about something that seems non-tangible? The group experience provided a trust-building environment that helped pave the way to creating an openness for spirituality growth.

How do you define spirituality?

- "Your feelings within yourself. How you interact and see the beauty in nature. How you interact with others."
- "There must be a creator, or how would grass grow green in the spring?"
- "Faith helps me to believe in the things I cannot see."
- "I cannot see my relationship with God, but I can feel it."
- "Healing in recovery is spiritual."
- "Spirituality for me is a balance of the mind, body, and spirit. It enhances the inner peace within me. It is the communication between my inner most spirit and something greater. I put my trust in this spirit."
- "Religion and the church is a big part of spirituality for me. Celebrating with other believers is necessary for me."

- "Spirituality is love. Anytime we love each other or experience the beauty around us, we are being spiritual."
- "I have a problem with someone telling me what my spirituality should be. If they do this, they have definitely crossed a line where they are not welcome. They have definitely crossed a boundary. My relationship or religious experience is mine."

Spirituality is a personal, indescribable relationship with something that is part of us, and yet greater than us. It is something that is experiential and developed over time.

How do you practice your spiritual beliefs?

- "I tried several religions until I found the right one."
- "You can have a relationship with God without going to church."
- "By praying in my own words, I have better communication with God. I try not to use the words of other men."
- "To me, it has always been me and nobody else. I do not believe in God."
- "Every Sunday, I flip through the television channels looking for TV evangelists. I'm trying to see if there are any messages for me in the programming."
- "Organized religion can be built on shame and guilt. I want a better relationship with God, one that is built on love and acceptance."

- "Getting in touch with nature, walking through the woods, and sitting by the river bank helps me get closer to God."
- "Having an open wood-burning fire helps me reflect and relax. It is meditative and soothing for me. My mind can wander without distraction."
- "Any style of music helps me to celebrate my relationship with God."
- "I always end my prayers with the prayer *The Lord's Prayer.*"

A man described how a Buddhist monk once said his spiritual practice was based on sitting, walking, and eating. Others questioned how this was different from what all of us do. We all sit, walk, and eat. What makes a monk different is that when he sits he knows he is sitting. When he walks, he knows he is walking. When he eats, he knows he is eating. Buddhists believe in practicing mindfulness each moment. They try to be aware of what is going on within themselves and their surroundings in the moment. Group members commented that their thoughts are often lost in the past by trying to make sense of unresolved issues or on future projects. Learning to spend more time in the present was a very refreshing concept. If we lose ourselves in the past, or future, we rob ourselves of the opportunity to enjoy the moment.

Some men felt that meditation brought them to a relaxing place that distanced them from their busy minds. The group mentioned various other ways they relaxed, such as: praying, walking in nature, sitting by an open fire, and listening to music. These activities helped them to take a break from the past and live in the moment.

Several men thought their experiences with organized religions were based on shame and guilt. They longed for a better relationship with God that was built on love and acceptance. Some participants felt they could have a connection with God without attending church and thought religion was a hindrance to their healing process. Others felt their organized religion was very instrumental in their healing process.

Looking for a religion can be a challenging task. Some people try several religions before becoming comfortable with their choice. Anyone wishing to pursue a religion may want to choose a church that provides an environment that does not resemble the abuse from the past. Choose a religion that encourages you to make your own choices. One that encourages positive self-esteem, and is not based on guilt and shame. These men wanted a sense of warmth, caring, and community.

Where do you presently see yourself with your spiritual views?

- "I feel like I am halfway there and trust God to bring me to the other half."
- "I am more conscious of my beliefs in God now than I ever was. I do not know what the future will bring."
- "I don't believe in God, although going to church may be something to try in the future. I'm curious to try something different. Things in the Bible do not make any sense to me. God cannot be proven scientifically."
- "I need God to listen to me and guide me."

- "I am just starting to explore what spirituality means to me."

- "The more I forgive myself, the closer I will be at accepting God into my life. I do not feel very loveable in God's eyes. I think I have failed God."

- "I need God to help me deal with one day at a time."

- "It is a slow continuous growth process that will last the rest of my life."

- "I am hopeful God will help me forgive myself for any guilt I am still carrying."

- "I need God to help me understand what spirituality means to me."

- "I hope I have the courage to explore my religious beliefs."

- "I can't have a relationship with God because I have too many problems of my own right now, problems that I feel I have no control over. At this time, I am not ready for God. I have problems with anybody or anything in any position of power, including God. My past is full of people in positions of power who have hurt me."

- "I am not ready to put God in my life. I will not pretend to love God when I do not. I'm not ready and will not put on a false face. Until I put some closure to the abuse, I will continue to carry a lot of hatred. Love left me when I was abused; my heart was ripped apart and torn away from me. Until I can get past this, I can't love God or anyone else."

Group members are reminded that they are exactly where they need to be in their spiritual journey. Their future choices are for them to decide, and they are responsible for choosing a direction that works best for them.

Where do you see yourself spiritually in the future?

- "I would like to be closer to God. I would like to have greater inner peace and accept the things I cannot change. God will help me cope with things in a healthier manner. I can see myself attending church, singing with fellow church members, interacting with others in a more confident manner, humming to myself, and smiling."

- "I will be more relaxed and balanced in mind, body, and spirit. I don't want to be a loner anymore. You will see me talking to others, pursuing a hobby, enrolling in a college course for seniors, doing public speaking on health and welfare issues, playing the keyboard, doing upholstery for fun, singing at church, and doing photography."

- "I can see myself spending more time reflecting on my life and choosing a path with spiritual input. I will be having more conversations with God and asking for clarification to my questions."

- "I am not sure what spirituality is or what my future will bring. I can see myself reaching out to others more often and giving more of myself. Some day, I may try to go to church. If love is God, then I must be somewhat spiritual."

When looking at another person's belief patterns, we try to stay away from black and white, good or bad, right or wrong thinking. There is no one, single, right way to be connected to your higher power. Spirituality is an individual, experiential journey that is developed over time. It is a process. As people work through their recovery, their views on spiritualism change. These men did not need any spiritual belief pattern to be part of the group. They can heal with or without a specific set of beliefs.

Has recovery hindered or strengthened your spirituality?

- "When I was sexually abused by a minister, I blamed myself and thought God would never be part of my recovery process. I thought I was totally on my own. I thought I could do it by myself. God eventually gave me the guidance to heal within. I could not recover totally with just the advice from men. I needed something greater."

- "God never forgets you; he helps me put the sexual abuse out of my mind at times and not dwell on it. I still dream about it, but I do not think about it all the time. By practising spirituality, I can see the beauty in the world."

- "By asking for guidance in my journey, I can focus on the present. God helps me prioritize what is important to me."

- "My spirituality was never hindered by the abuse. I knew my abuser would some day be held accountable. If the system does not get him, God will."

- "I never thought of including spirituality into my journey. Perhaps, I should give that some thought."

- "Someday, I want to go back to church, but I do not know if I am ready yet."

- "I used to be mad at everybody and everything, including God. I felt I was on my own, in a scary world. I still think that way at times."

- "I do not know if there is a God."
- "When I was sick, spirituality did not mean a lot to me. As I become healthier, the more important spirituality is to me."
- "I believe in the poem *Footprints*. This poem talks about a man looking back at his life as he walks along the beach. His spiritual journey represents his footprints and the footprints of God, side by side in the sand. In the most troubling times in his life, he noticed there was only one set of footprints in the sand. The man asks God, 'Why were you not there for me, when I needed you the most?' God replied, 'I was there, during your most troubling times. The reason there was only one set of foot prints is because I was carrying you.' God was there for me too when I needed him the most."
- "God has helped me put the abuse into a proper perspective. The abuse is not who I am. It is only something that has happened to me."
- "As I give up control, the closer I get to God."
- "Pain can be part of our spiritual growth. It seems the more pain I have in my life, the closer I get to God."

Various members mentioned that in the early stages of recovery, they felt themselves moving away from God. They the gap was widening, but as time evolved, they felt that gap closing. One man referred to a common saying in spirituality — we often have to be emptied before we can be filled.

If God loves, why does sexual abuse happen to children?

- "I do not practice spirituality; I can't understand why God let this happen to me."

- "Why did God let the sexual abuse happen to a defenseless boy? I got really angry at God and myself."

- "I used to blame myself, not God. I was mad at several people in the church for having an abuser for a minister."

- "Who would believe a minister in a high position of power would do this to a boy? But it was not God that caused the abuse. It was a man with a problem and other people chose not to help me."

- "My prayers and questions to God helped me realize he had nothing to do with what happened to me."

- "God does not let abuse happen. He is there with us throughout the abuse and helps with the recovery or rebuilding process."

- "I do not think I blame God, but I sure questioned why he did not help. This took me a long time to accept. At times, I still wonder."

- "I thought I lost my connection with God, thinking recovery was totally mine. I am glad that God is, and probably always was, a part of my life. I used to feel that God was against me. I thought the abuse was my fault and God would punish me. I now realize that God loves me unconditionally and the abuse is not my fault."

One man in the group talked about how God loves his people so much that he gives them "free will" to live on earth in a fashion of their choice. God does not condone the abuse of children, but His/Her spirit will be there for those that ask for help and guidance.

Do you have to forgive the abuser?

- "*The Lord's Prayer* wants us to 'forgive us our trespasses as we forgive those who have trespassed against us.' I have forgiven my abusers and will let God take care of dealing with them. This thought process developed over time, and I did not forgive the abuser for years. I still do not talk to the abuser and probably never will, but I do forgive him."

- "I like to think I have forgiven my abusers, but even now, I cannot stand the sight of a nun, even though I know not all nuns are abusive. I try to forgive, but that is hard."

- "You do not have to forgive people who have hurt you, but you should forgive yourself."

- "I can forgive the person, but I cannot forgive the behaviour. I hate their behaviour and probably always will."

- "I do not like the perpetrator and probably never will, but I accept the fact that he had a problem. I could not carry the anger I had towards him any longer."

- "When I forgave the person, I let go of a lot of my anger."

People do not have to forgive the person who abused them, and they can heal without forgiving. The option of whether to forgive or not forgive is an individual choice. If someone feels they want to forgive, they decide when the time is right. Forgiving is a process and this process takes time.

One member said he can forgive the person but he can not forgive the behaviour. He hated their behaviour and probably always will. Separating the person from the behaviour is not easy for anyone who has been hurt. Forgiving never means that you condone abusive behaviour. Sexual abuse and the exploitation of children are always wrong.

Many men talked about coming to a place of acceptance. They could not forgive the abuser, but they accepted the situation for what it was: an abnormal event happening to a good person. The energy needed to stay angry with the abuser can be exhausting. People often forgive as a means of honouring themselves and not as a method to appease the abuser. Some men talked about coming to an understanding that the abuser had mental health issues, and they accepted the fact this person had their own problems.

Separating the person from their behaviour is not an easy task. You can love the person and hate the behaviour. By learning to forgive, some folks let go of their anger, which they referred to as their own "living hell."

Being spiritual does not eliminate the stages of recovery and is not an alternative to grieving. The main reason for getting in contact with a higher power is to enhance healing, not to escape from the process.

Be aware of any religious leader who tells you they have the answers to all your problems. The best help was, and is, within you, and only you can choose a path that meets your needs. You can listen to others, educate yourself, and choose a direction that is best for you. The role of a support person, both spiritually and non-spiritually, is to accompany you on your journey, not to dictate their own views or direct you to follow their path.

Some men said they spent their whole lives searching outside of themselves for the answers to their problems. They were looking for that one person, or one thing, that could heal them, often searching from the outside-in. As they changed to a posture of searching from the inside-out, they obtained greater inner peace. Going inward can be a way of connecting to God. They were amazed that the answers to their questions were within them all along. Their own greatest resource was, and is, themselves. Nobody can do their work for them. No one can grieve and feel their losses for them. Others can provide support and information, but the work is theirs. This concept is not unique to male survivors but holds true for all individuals.

One man's search for God

Bill told this story five years after the group sessions had ended. He explained the effects of being sexually abused. Bill talked about his search for meaning and how his spirituality evolved over time. At the age of eight, his parents brought him to church every Sunday, and he eventually became an altar boy. He assisted the priest at Sunday gatherings, weddings, and funerals. Over a two-year span, he was sexually abused by his brother. This older sibling informed him that God approved of the sexual activity taking place.

Once Bill came to an understanding that the sexual attention was wrong, he questioned why God would allow such terrible things to happen to a small boy; especially one who helped out at Sunday mass. Bill wondered why God did not protect him and guide him through that troubling time. He also felt dirty and thought he must have done wrong in God's eyes. Bill had too many questions and not enough answers.

Most of the time, he sensed there was a God, but felt he did not belong with the chosen few that God loved. The fact that he was abused proved to him that he was not good enough to be protected, and was not worthy to be in God's family. His coping with the ripple effects of abuse included drinking, sex addictions, and an unhealthy lifestyle. This further reaffirmed his inability to be God-like. For the next twenty years, he distanced himself from organized religion and gave up on trying to live the life of a spiritual person. He could not forgive himself for his actions and could not understand a God that would allow him to be in such pain. He thought he was being punished.

After he consciously started a recovery process and went through a divorce, he continued to explore his relationship with a higher power. Bill thought his Catholic upbringing was based on shame and his longing for a spiritual connection would be rejected. He thought only perfect followers were worthy of God's love. Bill questioned if he had been brought up in the wrong religion. He started to read about other faiths, such as Buddhism, Judaism, and others. Bill found peacefulness in a transition that changed his looking at life from the outside-in to the inside-out. Meditation and mindfulness became a delightful way of enjoying solitude and having a connection with what he called the inner truth or a greater sense of reality.

Although Bill felt the presence of something greater than himself, he had tremendous feelings of guilt for his past actions. He tried desperately to be God-like but seemed to fail on a regular basis. This caused him to be sceptical, thinking he could never live up to God's expectations. Bill still longed for the Holy Spirit.

Several years passed, and he started studying his original Christian faith, but was confused. He liked some of the teachings this religion had to offer but also enjoyed various aspects of other religions or beliefs. While working through a depression, he telephoned for help. After various requests, he found a spiritual person who helped him sort through the "fog." Bill was taught that it is okay to explore various faiths as a method of choosing a path that would best meet his needs. God does not live in a "box," and it was good for him to allow the Holy Spirit to flow through him in his search.

Continually plagued with thoughts of other people in pain, he could not understand why any God would allow others to suffer in unfair ways. He learned that God created the world and gave it to man. Included in this gift was the offering of free will – an opportunity to live a life of their choice. Many people choose to live without any spiritual beliefs, and that is their choice to make. Bill learned that God does not intervene with our mistakes, but he is there to help us up when we fall. He/she does not want us to be like robots without choices. Bill said his higher power allows people to make choices, and some people choose to do terrible things to others, such as being sexually abusive.

Bill thought his relationship with God is similar to all his relationships on earth. All loving relationships have struggles, and they need effort to mature and grow. He said the biggest difference was that we can not measure God's love, and this love is beyond our human understanding. Bill's higher power does not work on a justice system, which includes crime and punishment. He works on a system of love and forgiveness. Bill learned that God does not like sin but loves the sinner. He said that all people are sinners and are not expected to be totally pure. Bill explained that God does not focus on our shortcomings but on how we try to be God-like. He knows we will fail at times, but he wants us to get up and applauds our efforts.

Prayer and meditation helped Bill come to a greater understanding of himself. He challenges others to actively work through concerns they may have with their higher power. He stresses that this may require airing your concerns in an argumentative fashion. Bill encourages us to give God our anger and tell him that you are mad at him. He said if you want a relationship with God, you have to work through your problems with him or her. Remember, if you do not ask questions you do not get the answers.

Bill's last point was to look for God in a peaceful, restful way. He said the joy is in the journey and not the destination. When Bill focused too much on the destination, he could not recognize the teachings along the way. Bill was reminded of some comments made in group, such as: less can be more, and you can not make a flower grow by pulling on it. Bill finds himself pleased with his Christian beliefs, and he's delighted with the teachings from other religions as well.

People who have travelled this far have fought a long, strenuous and rewarding journey. Moving into the last stage of recovery is a celebration of growth and learning to maintain new skills.

Stage #10: Moving On

Life after group

Approaching the final session of group can be filled with a lot of tension. The topic of moving-on creates many mixed emotions within the participants. They often feel excited, enlightened, insightful, and confident. Simultaneously, they can feel vulnerable, nervous, and uneasy. Members talk about being unsure of themselves and how they are concerned about the new challenges they will face in their future.

Men have many questions about what life will look like after group. They wonder: When will I be home free? When I have completed group, will my recovery be completed? When can I put this behind me? What does moving on look like? How will I know if I am ready to move on? Can I handle life without this group? What will another group be like? Should I join another group? Should I continue with individual counselling?

The end of group is not the ending of new growth. It is the beginning of something greater, a new part of life that includes new opportunities and new challenges. These men are equipped with new perspectives and objectives. Moving on is an evolution to a higher level of awareness. The participants have a better understanding of how the sexual abuse has influenced their lives and what they can do as individuals to influence their future.

Many men find their group experience to be one of the most enriching aspects of their healing journey. Sexual abuse is too complex for any victim to resolve in ten short weeks. Most group members received individual counselling over an extended period of time prior to group, and some of them continued throughout their group experience. Within several weeks of one group ending, another one usually begins. Each participant is given an opportunity to join the new group. Every person is unique in the number of groups they wished to participate in. Some men prefer participating in one to three separate groups, others prefer to stay longer. All men were given opportunities to continue their healing process with individual counselling and/or new groups. Some men recognized the need for extended support and talked about forming their own long-term groups with selected members.

Group appears to be part of a logical progression for men. Most men start their recovery or journey in secrecy and isolation. This progresses to telling someone, and perhaps signing up for individual counselling. Once a person feels comfortable talking about their situation, they may join a support group. Group provides a safe and supportive environment to develop the skills needed for the next logical progression, redefining interactions within their families and communities without therapy. Although this progression is noticeable, it is not a linear process. Survivors may be involved in individual counselling, group, and be redefining their relationship with their communities all at the same time.

From the first session, group members are encouraged to anticipate life after group and take proactive measures to prepare for their future. They support each other in identifying and working on the skills needed to enhance their interactions with others. These men plan for their future by setting obtainable goals. These goals need to be very concrete and specific, giving them a tool by which to measure their successes.

One group member mentioned that his goal was to step out of isolation. The group asked him to be clearer and make his desired outcome more measurable. He was going to walk every morning, visit a friend at least once a week, attempt to interact with new people whenever possible, and see a counsellor once a month to help him stay focused. These goals were very specific and gave him a method to evaluate his progress.

It was important for these men to discuss the ending of group throughout the ten-week process. Members needed to think about life after group and put their experiences into a healthy perspective. In the first session, they learned that group had a definite beginning and ending point, and it was important to building support systems outside of our meeting place. One goal is preparing for life after group. The men talked about what they hoped to gain from their experience and how this would benefit them after the ten sessions had been completed.

Throughout the ten sessions, common themes naturally led into a conversation about healthy termination. One of the most common themes was when people become too dependent on each other, and they started talking about an elevated need for group. The men needed to feel supported but not be overly dependent on each other. They needed to celebrate how each of them assisted each other, and at the same time, work towards developing their individual support system outside of the group.

Some men commented that group represented the family they never had, the family they wished they had. Even though the support from each other provides understanding, compassion, and the acceptance they may not have received in their families, it is not their family and should not be seen as a replacement. Groups are designed to have an end. What they learn from each other would be beneficial for a lifetime. Men were encouraged to talk about how their interactions with each other resembled the family they wish they had.

Participants talked about their fears of becoming too dependant on each other. They did not want this experience to represent another situation in their lives where they got too close to somebody, expressed their vulnerabilities, and were left feeling abandoned. Men discussed the difference between past feelings of abandonment, and the ending of group. This helped them prepare for the end of those meetings and at the same time resolved any feelings and emotions connected to past unresolved issues. Men often developed friendships throughout the group process that continued on after the group ended. One of their goals was to live life without group and be more self-sufficient.

If the ending of group is seen as something negative, these men would have lost motivation. But if the last session was seen as the beginning of something greater, they gained momentum and motivation. This motivation was needed to carry them into the next stage of their lives, which included family, friends, and their community.

When "moving on," participants have a good awareness of their past, including how it affected them in the present. They knew where they presently were, and where they wanted to go. Not only did they know where they were trying to go, they knew how to identify it once they got there. This is why it was so important to be specific and concrete with goal setting. One person talked about how critical it is for him to be true to himself by "being real." He would achieve that goal by spending some time each day reflecting on himself and writing his thoughts into a journal. After gaining clarity from his writing experiences, he would share his feelings openly with safe and supportive people. He could then measure his success by asking himself if he was performing the activities outlined in his goal setting.

What does moving on look like?

- "I will deal with every situation as it arises and grieve losses as they occur."
- "Not buying into my old dysfunctions and negative ways of thinking."
- "Use my energy to work on myself and not the people around me. I cannot change others; I can only change myself."
- "I will take what I have learned in counselling and group and apply it to my life in my community."

- "Build and maintain a healthy support team. I will build relationships with people I can trust, and I'll work hard to keep these relationships healthy."
- "I will continually work towards a balanced lifestyle."
- "Remember the serenity prayer."
- "I have come a long way and have learned a lot. I want to pass on some of this knowledge to others. I want to help all survivors and be true to myself by being real."
- "Recognize that all feelings and emotions can be an opportunity for growth. This can be an exciting journey. Anything I experience gives me more insight into myself."
- "Growth is like travelling through a dark tunnel. When you see and experience the light at the end, you do not want go back into the darkness of the tunnel. I will strive to move constantly towards that light."
- "By working from the inside-out rather than the outside-in; I will be proactive rather than reactive."
- "I cannot remove all the stress in my life. Recovery is constantly developing tools to work through these stresses as they happen."
- "By continually recognizing and accepting that I am a worthwhile person."
- "I am changing my focus from 'I do not have a future' to 'there is hope.' I have an influence in the direction I travel through life. It feels good to be moving towards something. This makes life worth living."
- "We need to remember that the abuse is something that happened to us. Never confuse who we are with what happened to us. The

abuse and the effects are only a small portion of who we are."

- "I have learned to let go of a lot of my past. I cannot stay angry and sad forever."
- "I recognize and celebrate my growth. I like to remember how far I have travelled."

It is important to remember that abuse is something that happens to people, and not to confuse who you are with what happens to you. The abuse and the effects were only a small portion of who they are. One of the first things these participants learned was to never confuse the abnormality of the abuse with the abnormality of self. What happened to them was abnormal. It was wrong and it never should have happened, but they are very "normal." The various ways they learned to cope with the abuse were very normal responses to very abnormal situations. It was important to separate the abuse from the individuality of the person. Many men saw the abuse as their identity: the core of who they are. As these men evolved, they saw the abuse as something that had happened to them. It was no longer all consuming and was only a part of their past that did not take up every ounce of their energy.

Members recognized and celebrated their growth, remembering how far they had travelled. It is important for group members to celebrate their successes with each other. Sometimes other participants noticed changes in one other that the individual did not recognize.

Participants could not, and can not, remove all the stress in their life. Recovery includes constantly developing tools to work through these stresses as they happen. These men learned to transform the troublesome parts of their lives into a more positive and functional way of living. By learning to grieve unresolved issues from their past, they developed the skills needed to grieve current losses as they occur.

They described their feelings and emotions as an opportunity for new growth, as part of an exciting journey. Things they experienced gave them more insight into themselves. By living more consciously and being aware of themselves, they could choose how they wanted to interact with their surroundings. In the past, some men believed vulnerable feelings and emotions should be avoided at all costs. By changing their perspectives, they opened themselves up to being more "real" with themselves and their surroundings. They now view their feelings as an opportunity instead of a weakness.

Many men had a burning desire to help others. As one man stated, he had come a long way and had learned a lot. He wanted to pass on his knowledge and help other survivors. The energy once needed to cope can now be channelled into living, and perhaps engaging in activities that allow some positive meaning to come from their pain. These men felt proud that their comments in this book will be of some help to others.

There is a shortage of accurate, reliable information for the public and health professionals on male sexual abuse recovery issues. Men who have undergone the process of healing are the experts, and they are the best teachers to educate both the public and professionals. Some men found comfort in volunteering for organizations that lobbied governments to be more responsive to the needs of victims.

There are many ways to help others, but they were careful not to do this prematurely. If they rushed to the aid of others before they did their own work, they would have hindered their own recovery and may not have been effective in helping others. Helping others prematurely can be a way of avoiding their own pain. It can seem much easier to deal with other people's problems than it is to face their own. They needed to take care of their own needs; there was plenty of time to help others later. By establishing a good foundation for themselves, they were better able to attend to the needs of others. They tried to focus on "walking the walk" and not just "talking the talk."

Group members would refer to the abuser as the "ghost from the past," as if they were struggling with something that was not real. They may not have been in physical danger, but their minds could still be haunted by past memories. Men were asked to challenge this ghost from the past and ask themselves what is different now. As men evolved, they learned to spend more time in the present and not get lost in a "time zone" from the past. As they moved on, they learned to put much of their past behind them, but they could only do this when they were ready.

Part of healing includes knowing when to let go, and members could not predict when this might be. Letting go is important because people do not want to stay angry and sad forever. One member said he experienced a lot of painful feelings but tried not to rush them. At a point in time these feelings stabilized, and he felt more secure and grounded. This is not the end of the line for him, but he had broken out of isolation from the past, learned to treat himself well in the present, and is committed to moving in a positive direction for the future.

To be truly content, men need to be comfortable with who they are. They questioned each other when trying to define the inner peace they all strove for. They have the freedom to be themselves, and they recognize that this freedom comes from within. Freeing themselves from unhealthy patterns from the past was a huge step in the right direction.

By establishing a positive connection with themselves, they were creating a solid foundation for future growth. One of the key elements in the later stages of recovery was gaining an influence over themselves, and at the same time, giving up control. They learned that they cannot control everything and everyone around them. Total control is an illusion. Life is mysterious, and true joy is learning to live in this mystery.

Group members have learned that they may not be able to change others, but they can change themselves. These men have experienced greater success and satisfaction when they focused on their own growth. Men in group often learn to accept themselves for who they are, warts and all.

Participants want their futures to include a healthy support team. Questions they asked themselves included: Am I able to receive and give support? Can I set healthy boundaries for myself in relationships with others? Am I able to express my feelings to my support team? Do I express my anger in a positive manner that is not destructive to me or those around me? Can I trust others when appropriate? Do I know when I am in a toxic relationship? Do I know how to change or terminate toxic relationships? Do I have the skills to build and maintain relationships with people I can trust?

In the first session of a group, one member said he could not wait to be done talking about all his feelings so life could get back to normal. This man later realized that "normal" from the past was not such a great place, and that his old views on masculinity had hindered his growth. Being ready to leave group did not mean he was totally autonomous or invulnerable. Good mental health is not the absence of stress; it is dealing with concerns as they happen.

There is no specific moment in time when the sexual abuse recovery process ends. The last stage of recovery is the rest of their lives. The most common concern for these men was the search for a meaningful connection. They wanted to have positive interactions with themselves, others, and their surroundings. If men are searching for positive connections, then moving on must include establishing, maintaining, and nurturing these connections. As a person advances towards positive connections, he moves further away from isolation.

Moving on can be part of a transition towards healthy masculinity. The ideal healthy man is first and foremost a human being who is not afraid to look at himself. He is a man who tries to be aware of where he is going; he is not afraid to let others know his feelings; he tries to be respectful, understanding, compassionate, and kind; he tries to relate well with other men and can be content with his masculinity.

Life is good.

Part # 3

Information for Partners, Family, and Friends

This chapter is written to help people who have relationships with men who have experienced childhood sexual abuse. Very little information is available for partners, loved ones, friends, and family members. The information provided here will help others to define their role as a positive, healthy support person.

In the following pages, group members talk about the collective denials of their community and what they wished their families would have told them as children, followed by advice on how families can help now. Participants discuss how their families of origin were an obstacle in their recovery process and how they overcame these hurdles. The term "father hunger" is introduced, plus rules to consider when communicating with partners. A member tells a story about how healing contributed to the break-up of his marriage.

As a society, people tend to suffer from what is called "collective-denial." They do not want to believe that terrible things, such as sexual abuse, happen in their own communities, particularly not in their own families. Participants discussed how their families went to great lengths to avoid the topic all together. They wanted so desperately to be believed, while their families, or the people they loved, wanted to think these awful things did not happen. They needed to talk and be heard, but their families wished to avoid the topic completely.

The men who sought support were abused ten, twenty, thirty, or forty years ago. For some men, it was the first time in their lives that they were talking about what happened to them as children. Dealing with their past sexually abusive experiences was very sensitive for them and for their loved ones. Unfortunately, many families did not remain intact throughout this trying time and most members had similar patterns with their loved ones. When they first reached for help, they were not happy with the responses they received. Frustrations built up and they temporarily separated from their families to develop a greater sense of self. Some participants rejoined their families; however others are still maintaining their distance. Few people stayed in close contact throughout their healing journey. Each member regretted the distance that was put between themselves and their families. They also acknowledged they could not have resolved certain issues without some sort of temporary separation.

These men were in turmoil and were trying to make sense of a very complex part of their past. It was uncharacteristic for these men to reach out for support, and it was, and is, even more uncommon for our society to provide the necessary assistance. Even though the healing process is very difficult, it could be an opportunity for everyone involved to learn and grow together.

It was very moving when the men in group talked about their childhoods. When the group was asked what they wished their families would have said to them as children, you could feel the emotional energy in the room, and a sense that the entire group was moving back in time.

What do you wish your family would have told you as a child?

- "We are behind you."
- "Don't worry about it; we will take care of it for you."
- "We will provide safety for you."
- "You will be okay; it was not your fault."
- "I wanted to be touched in a loving way."
- "Anything positive would have been nice. There was nothing positive."
- "I love you."
- "I'm proud of you."
- "If ever you have a problem, come to us."
- "I was real suicidal when I was twelve, any positive comment would have made a difference."

When the men from group looked back at their childhoods, they expressed a void or empty feeling. As children, they wanted their loved ones to give them the positive affirmations they so desperately needed. As adults, they still needed these encouraging comments from the people they cared about. They were not asking for answers, they were searching for love, acceptance, reassurance, and safety.

It can be difficult for friends and family to cope with someone who has experienced any form of sexual violence. Internal conflict may arise when loved ones feel they don't have the skills to adequately assist the victim. Very few people are educated on sexual abuse recovery, and the thought of supporting someone as they go through this trying time can seem overwhelming. Family and friends are often viewed as secondary victims. Even though they may not have been personally involved in the initial abusive situation, they still experience much pain and discomfort associated with their loved ones' recovery processes. The men acknowledged that their loved ones needed to be supported throughout this stressful time, but they did not have the emotional energy because of their own pain. Support people need to take care of themselves, and this may include asking for help so that they can maintain their health. The group had some comments about how support people could have helped them.

What can family and friends do to help?

- "I just wanted my family to listen to me."
- "Families and friends should not try to change me."
- "I wish they would have said, 'Call me anytime, whenever you are having a problem.'"
- "I want others to try and understand me."
- "Accept me for the way I am. Do not be judgmental. They cannot talk me out of recovery."
- "Just be there for me, and give opinions only when asked."
- "It would be nice if everyone just loved each other."
- "If only they would believe me and show some interest in my pain. They can't make my pain go away by telling me, 'It happened a long time ago' or, 'Just try and forget it.' When they say that, I feel worse."

- "I want to be respected as a human being."
- "Let me make my own decisions and grieve at a pace I am comfortable with."
- "They need to know that I cannot get over this in a short period of time; I wish I could."

Survivors are looking for non-judgmental acceptance and understanding. These men do not want to be pushed. Gentle motivation, once in a while, might be helpful, but loved ones need to be careful when advising someone how they should proceed. Most people in recovery are seeking validation, not recommendations.

Grieving takes time, and the survivor will need time and space to grow. Participants mentioned that they mostly needed somebody that would listen to them, somebody they could share their stories with. They were not looking for answers. They just wanted an opportunity to express their feelings and emotions. The men in group talk about a search for acceptance and how they felt uneasy when criticized. Participants felt anxiety when they sensed they were being patronized. Support persons may wish to consider that these men are not at their best when working through past issues. They are trying to regain a sense of balance and control over their lives.

Members learned that it was difficult for others to be empathetic and how loved ones may struggle with trying to imagine themselves in the victim's position. They recognize how others must have had difficulty understanding what they were going through. One person made a valid point when stating that people do not have to be a sexual abuse survivor to be supportive. The support person may not have had similar experiences as the victim, but if they could think of a time in their lives when they experienced fear, confusion, humiliation, or isolation, it would help them to understand part of what the victim was experiencing.

More than anything else, these men wanted to be understood, and they felt they would have reacted more favourably if responded to in a sensitive and receptive fashion. They mentioned that it would be nice if others did not judge, blame, criticize, or compare them to others. Support people can help by communicating with caring words and a positive attitude.

At a time when these men were challenging their own thought patterns, they so desperately wanted others to believe them, not just about being sexually abused, but how it was affecting their lives. Members sensed that others did not believe them, and they hesitated sharing, for fear of not being supported. The words "I believe you," and "it's not your fault" may be the most important words someone can say to survivors.

These men were trying to find a voice that had been silent for many years. At first, they wished they would have been able to keep silent and forget, but they could not. The cost of secrecy was greater than the risk of reaching out. It was quite a challenge for them to talk about the situations they had tried so hard to forget, especially when they sensed others did not want to hear them anyways.

Knowing when, or if, to talk about the past with friends and loved ones was not a simple task. Survivors were faced with many challenges when choosing who and to what degree they were willing to share their past experiences. Men were often sceptical when making this important decision, thinking, who would be the right person? How much could they share with that person? When was the right time? What was the proper way of sharing? Would they be accepted or rejected? It was also very challenging for them and their support people to balance healing and living. Although recovery is very emotionally draining for everyone involved, the stresses of regular life continue and need to be dealt with at the same time.

It was very important that family members recognize the huge level of trust these people were placing in them when they shared sensitive details about their past abusive experience, especially since these men have had negative experiences with trust in their past.

How has your family of origin been an obstacle in your recovery process?

- "My parents were always critical of anything I did. Now I am critical of myself in everything I do. It feels like I am always beating myself up."
- "I saw my parents acting out their anger by hurting others, and I was determined never to do that. I did not know how to express my anger. I swallowed my pain by never expressing myself."
- "My family asks so many difficult questions. These questions leave me feeling that they think

it was my fault, that I somehow wanted to be abused."

- "Sometimes there is confusion as to where I want to grow, compared to how my family wants me to proceed."
- "There was always an emotional distance between myself and my family."
- "Dad was totally out of control, destroying things. I destroyed myself, but I do not destroy others or property. I do anything possible to address the fears of others so that they will not be out of control."
- "Silence and secrecy has always been cherished by my family and society. What about my needs?"

Group members talked about the pain of feeling judged and interrogated when talking about the trauma they experienced. They found certain questions to be offensive, such as: Why did that happen to you? Did you do anything to provoke him or her? That was a long time ago, why don't you just forget about it? Why think about it now? Why don't you just get over it? Be a man and don't let it bother you. Participants mentioned how their families asked so many difficult questions that left them feeling the abuse was their fault and that somehow they wanted to be abused.

How did you overcome family of origin obstacles?

- "Have realistic expectations from the family and people you disclose to, remember they are dealing with their own insecurities surrounding the sexual abuse. We deserve and need support, but we must also realize we will not always get it. As we travel through our grieving processes, we can expect that many of our present friends will not support us throughout our journeys."

- "By setting healthy boundaries with all the people I interact with. My parents did not have any boundaries. "
- "By realizing I was not responsible for my parents rage."

It would have been more helpful if these men had had the support of their families, but all too often that was not the case, and the vast majority of men do not. They longed to have someone believe them and care about them. They needed to hear that they were not crazy, that they were having common reactions to a horrible experience. Support people are encouraged to express that there is a way through the pain and that they have confidence the men will make it to the other side.

During one group session, a member asked for some input to help him define the type of relationship he could obtain with his mother. Jim stated that he was depressed about a situation with his mother and siblings. He said, "I am angry with her, and we have not spoken for some time now. She refuses to be a healthy member of my support team. Both her and my siblings will not discuss anything about the sexual abuse I experienced as a child by the family minister. I have no contact with her at the moment, and even though I want a relationship with her, she will never change. The other day I saw a car drive by that resembled her vehicle, and I immediately got angry. Why is this and what can I do about it? The group talked about something the other day—that many survivors choose to have a superficial relationship with their family of origin. Can we talk about that again?"

Jim identified that seeing a car resembling his mother's triggered his anger and rage. This anger gave him insight into unresolved issues within their relationship. He missed not having her in his life and felt his children might benefit from a relationship with their grandmother. He was bitter about his past and sceptical about his future interactions with his mom.

The men started with favourite sayings from the group, "You cannot change others; you can only change yourself" and, "You are responsible for your feelings and emotions; and others are responsible for theirs." After some discussion, Jim identified that his anger was a personal obstacle to overcome. His displeasure, although justifiable, may be an obstacle to having any type of future relationship with his mother or siblings.

Jim realized that he did not like his past position in the family or the personal price he had to pay to keep that role. There was an unwritten rule that he was to keep silent about his feelings and emotions, even if that was harmful to his growth as an individual. It was very important for him to break the family cycle and develop newer, healthier patterns of behaviour. In Jim's case, he needed some time and distance from his family to sort through his thoughts and feelings. Jim may decide to keep silent about the sexual abuse when dealing with the family, but that does not mean he has to be speechless outside the family environment.

Family members often face their own insecurities when talking about sexual abuse. This is a difficult topic for them to discuss, and silence may be their way of protecting themselves from some difficult feelings. These men need to do what they need to do, for themselves. The group felt Jim should not try to fix his mother or his family and not engage in conversations that will not change the situation. Get the joys you can from the relationship, but do not try to fix the mess. He is not the therapist for his family and may choose to depersonalize and be superficial with them. Families rarely heal the past as a unit. The group wondered if the energy Jim spent on trying to change his family may not serve a better purpose by working on himself. Family members may want the same thing the survivor is looking for, an opportunity to choose how they run their own lives.

Group members were concerned that Jim's anger kept the old relationship pattern alive and hindered the possibility of a new one. They talked about various ways that Jim might be able to work through his anger. Often, where there is anger, there is also underlying hope of possible resolution. Unless Jim works through his anger and possibly some depression, he may never come to a place of acceptance for a new family relationship. He does not have a supportive family and may never have. He could grieve this loss and move towards redefining his new role within the family. The family may never engage in a deep caring conversation with him about his sexual abuse recovery. Jim was considering the following options: have a superficial relationship with his family; not have any contact with them; not have contact until he can sort through his feelings and emotions; keep trying to change them; or redefine the relationship in some other fashion.

Jim was automatically working at redefining his relationship with his mother by having this discussion with the group. As a child and in earlier adulthood, Jim was not allowed to challenge the unwritten rules of the family. One of those rules was "never question the family dynamics" and accept things the way they always have been. As a child, Jim was not encouraged to express his feelings and emotions openly. He felt his role was to be seen and not heard. The relationship between himself and his parents was very superficial. Everything appeared to be fine on the surface, but there was a void when it came to any emotional connection. As Jim grew as a person and started to live more consciously, he wanted to develop an emotional connection that was missing when he was younger. One problem may be that his mother may be unable to make this connection and perhaps was giving an honest effort to the best of her abilities. Jim is learning to get his needs met in new ways, and with other people.

Many participants spent enormous amounts of energy trying to change their families, hoping to educate them on sexual abuse recovery issues, longing to be validated and accepted, wanting their families to acknowledge their pain and celebrate their growth. Eventually, many men gave up on this goal and focused on their own inner healing.

Some members developed better relationships with their family of origin without discussing their sexual abuse. They gave up on trying to reach the emotional connection that seemed unattainable, but they maintained a relationship that included contact. They learned to go to the movies and laugh, to talk about the weather, to attend a sporting event, and even to get together on holidays and other events without the expression of deep inner feelings. As many people do, they learned to get their deeper needs met in other places. This may be a key reason why support groups were so important for these men.

Jim was developing new ways of communicating with others. He was working at setting boundaries and redefining his role in his family of origin. His "old role" of keeping silent about his inner feelings no longer worked for him, but it was familiar. He had limitations in how he expressed himself to his childhood family, but he could choose how he related to others as an adult. It took him over thirty years to learn the old way. Giving up on those old patterns did not happen overnight. The group understood that this is a difficult decision that only Jim could make. They supported him on whatever direction he chose.

The discussion about Jim ended, and the group changed the focus of conversation to their relationships with their fathers. It is quite common for the group members to jump from one topic to another. There is often something said by one person that triggers the thoughts of another. When one issue is addressed to satisfaction, the opportunity arises for someone else to speak.

Very few survivors talked about a positive, nurturing relationship with their fathers. The tension and energy levels seemed to mount whenever the groups talked about "father hunger." The vast majority of these men wished they had a better emotional connection with their fathers. It is perhaps important to note that none of the survivors in this group were sexually abused by their fathers.

What comes to mind when you hear the term "father-hunger"?

- "I do not watch television programs with father and son scenes. It hurts too much. I change the channel."
- "I can watch father and son themes now and not be torn apart."
- "My father was never a positive role model. In the past, I was always disappointed when searching for male mentors."
- "It was a real relief for me when my dad said 'I was too hard on you as a child.' It's too bad he had to wait until he was dying to say that."
- "I long for a relationship with my father but do not know how to obtain one."
- "When I think of what I needed from my father, I think of my lost childhood. I feel like the best of me was left back with that child. I often wonder what life would be like if I had been given more positive experiences throughout my childhood. "

Group members talked about the loss they felt from not having a supportive relationship with their fathers and what that loss meant to them. By having conversations about their dads, they recognized unhealthy patterns that existed between themselves and their own children. The group provided each other with support and encouragement to make healthy changes.

Many men said their fathers never told them they were proud of them or praised them with becoming respectable men. I could feel the energy in the room swell when fellow group members told each other that they were good men. Men need to hear this from their support teams. It is important to mention that everyone in group, at some level, enjoyed being praised by each other, but they also recognized that praise can be part of a superficial relationship. What they wanted most from each other was acceptance and honest feedback, recognizing that their feelings of self worth came mostly from within. The group often talked about working from the inside-out and how necessary it was for them to be personally proud of themselves.

There are a lot of men that wish or long for a positive connection with their fathers. Research seems to show that many fathers long for a better relationship with their sons, and that both could benefit from the love and support of each other. Group members talked sceptically, but affectionately, when entertaining the thought of improving their relationship with their fathers and mothers.

One member talked about the problems he encountered when communicating with his dad. They used to yell and scream at each other, and he found himself reacting the same way with his partner. He felt badly about that and asked the group for some guidelines to help him resolve their conflict in a non-violent way.

What are some positive rules to consider when communicating with your partner?

- "Talk to each other, and express your own feelings and emotions."
- "Respect each other as individuals."

- "Learn how to argue and solve problems peacefully."
- "Respect each other as equal parents. Do not undermine each other."
- "Talk about problems as they come up."
- "Learn to listen."
- "Learn to stand up for yourself and set healthy boundaries."

When they experienced conflict with their partners, they hoped to keep their residual anger separate from their reactive anger. They learned that their partners were not responsible for the pain they suffered as a child and how their pain connected to past events contributed to a large reservoir of residual anger that needed to be expressed. Residual anger usually surfaced in a place these people felt the safest, and unfortunately, that was within their family home. They are working to find new ways to release their anger without attaching it to reactive anger towards their partners. It was not fair to their partner if they reacted to a situation in the present and included their anger from the past. Their partner can love them and support them, but their loved ones can not take ownership of their feelings and emotions. Only they can do that. Open communication was so important between these men and their partners, and often, that had not been established. This became another task of recovery.

One member mentioned how important it was to set healthy boundaries for himself and also to respect the boundaries of his partner. Learning to communicate and honour their individual needs was a sign of respect for the other person's diversities.

One person talked about how he had been totally honest with his wife regarding the effects sexual abuse had on his life. He was ambivalent about sharing that with her but felt she was trustworthy. He told her not only about the abuse, but also the embarrassing ways he had coped with the memories from the past. As he worked on his recovery, there seemed to be a direct correlation between his getting healthier and the relationship growing further apart. The healthier he became, the worse the relationship got. Several years later, they separated and she immediately went to his family and exposed the secrets he had shared with her in trust. By enhancing some of the stories, she gained their approval and widened the gap between him and his family. This man felt his ex-partner used these trusted comments as a way to cover up her own inadequacies in the relationship. Since he had already had some concerns with his childhood family, she could buy into their dysfunctions and make herself look good. It worked for her but devastated him. He explained that he needed to tell someone about his past, but unfortunately chose the wrong person. What bothered him most were the feelings of betrayal. This breach of trust resembled feelings of betrayal from the past. Other members mentioned how hard it was to find safe and supportive people, and unfortunately some partners may not be in the safe category. Luckily, this man continued on his quest and found people who were safe to confide in. He wished he could have worked through his issues with his ex-wife, but he likes the person he is now and would not have wanted to stay unhealthy in order to keep the old relationship alive.

Many survivors find it beneficial to look at the distribution of power within the family and determine if each person has an opportunity to express themselves in an open respectable fashion. Some members found they were overly controlling, but most found they were being overly controlled. Some men felt powerless when they tried to give up controlling behaviours, and others felt helpless when faced with the controlling behaviours of their partners. Both partners are more likely to change if they feel confident that they will retain the respect and love of each other in the process.

Information for Support People and Counsellors

How to be an effective support person

Working with sexual abuse survivors is very difficult, and few people have specialized training for dealing with male victims. Be easy on yourself, and if you are unsure of how to proceed, at least do no harm.

The aim of a support person is to be very supportive and person-centred. Most men have everything within themselves to heal. What they need is a benevolent witness — somebody who can play their stories back to them. One of the nicest moments for a survivor is when the listener has an understanding of their stories.

The helper's role is to ask questions more than it is to give answers. Often, caregivers have their own beliefs about what is best for another individual, however, what works for one person does not necessarily work for another.

Individuals need to work and experience their own recovery process. By learning to trust their own inner wisdom, they move closer to their true self. A support person's role is to accompany men on their journeys and not take control of the trip. Victims are responsible for choosing their own path and deciding how fast they want to travel.

Each person is unique in how he makes sense of his experiences. No two recovery processes are the same.

Some people see a helper's role as someone who tells the person hurting what is best for them. I tend to disagree with this approach. The journey must be survivor-directed. Sexual abuse often creates a sense of being powerless, and the journey is about regain a sense of control.

Think of two people in an automobile: the helper is the passenger and the person seeking help is the driver. Sometimes the car gets stuck and the passenger has to get out and give a push to get the wheels rolling, but when the car starts moving, the driver controls the wheel.

Try to remove any imbalances of power between the helper and the person requesting assistance. There should be no hierarchies in the process; two people are simply learning from each other. At times, the helper is the teacher, and at other times, he/she is the student. They both learn and grow together. Remember, the person seeking help knows more about his experience than anyone else.

People are responsible for their own feeling and emotions and need to take ownership for the healing process. They need to take responsibility for their own lives, and others should not impede on that. Even though the survivor has everything within them to heal, others can provide an environment that will help foster this healing.

Self-empowerment is an essential part of the healing process. Many men feel shame when they talk about past coping skills. These coping skills were not entirely negative. We need to give people credit for their creativity and the ability to choose a skill that brought them to where they are right now; and where they are now is exactly where they need to be. The fact that they are talking about their struggles is a sign of strength and courage. Their past coping skills served a purpose; it kept them alive.

People seeking help are sharing very intimate details about their lives. A support person may be the first person in the world they ever talked to about very vulnerable concerns. They put their trust in the listener, and this trust should not be taken lightly. Confidentiality is a very important and part of trust building. There may be times when suicide is a possibility, and the survivor may need someone to take action on their behalf. Safety is always the number one priority.

The expression of feelings and emotions is essential in the healing process. Listening in a supportive way gives validation to these men's comments. People in pain wish to be accepted in the present moment. They want to be loved and accepted, just the way they are.

Most men want to recover from a purely intellectual perspective. They want to think their way through recovery, but unfortunately healthy grieving does not work that way. Experiencing feelings internally is an essential part of the grieving process that helps men gain insight into themselves. This insight gives them opportunities for transformation and integration. Adult survivors are experiencing feeling and emotions in the present they were not given an opportunity to experience as a child.

There is no need for forced disclosures. Gentle motivation may be necessary, but the survivor determines when they are ready to talk about important issues from their past. If someone never wishes to talk about the abuse, that choice must be respected. Survivors find it very unattractive when people ask for exact details about the abuse. The listener does not need to know every detail; however, it is important for men to have an opportunity to express how they feel about what happened.

Even if you think you understand the survivor's issues, it is important for men to be able to tell their stories. These stories may need to be told again and again. When survivors tell their story, they gain a better understanding of their past and the feelings and emotions they have connected to these stories.

Choose a safe and supportive location where the person feels comfortable spending time. This would be a location where they can be "comfortably" uncomfortable. If the person is not uncomfortable at times, they are probably not doing the work that needs to be done for personal growth. One man mentioned in the second session of a group that he felt very uncomfortable, but he was happy to be in an environment where he could work through his discomfort.

Tips to consider when counselling male survivors

Men from group determined the top fifteen points for a counsellor to consider when providing services to male sexual abuse survivors.

1. Survivors are the experts on their own sexual abusive experiences.

2. Listening and asking appropriate questions are more important than speaking.

3. Care about the people seeking help.

4. The counselling room must be warm and inviting.

5. Eliminate hierarchies, and remove any variables that may suggest a power imbalance.

6. Portray equality and see each other eye-to-eye.

7. Your clients have personal power and control; the direction they choose is theirs.

8. Be well-educated on recovery issues.

9. Motivate men towards self-empowerment.

10. Encourage men to disclose at a pace they are comfortable with.

11. Be open-minded and non-judgmental towards the coping skills of the men seeking help.

12. Believe in your clients and see the good in every one of them.

13. Honour the importance of the client/counsellor relationship.

14. Understand sexual abuse as a systemic problem and not just an individual mental health issue.

15. Accompany survivors on their journeys; do not create one for them.

The above tips are worth considering. They are based on removing hierarchies and honouring the individual seeking help. By following the above suggestions, the chances of the caregiver/survivor relationship being successful is greatly enhanced.

The masculinity exercise and anger journal that follow will assist in helping survivors become aware of their how they respond to their environment. The masculinity exercise was mentioned previously in the book, but it is worth repeating.

Counsellors will find this a helpful tool for facilitating positive change.

Masculinity Exercise

1. What did you learn about "being a man" from your family of origin and the culture you live in?

2. What labels are placed on men that step outside of these teachings?What labels are placed on men that step outside of these teachings?

3. How do you define healthy masculinity?

Anything learned can be unlearned. When people become aware of how they respond to anger, it gives them an opportunity to try different ways of responding. The anger journal is a helpful awareness tool for anyone wishing to make positive changes.

Anger journal

This simple journal provides a measurable tool for change. The person completing the form circles the level of intensity from 1 to 10. One would indicate mild intensity, while 10 would indicate a full blown rage. They explain the situation that sparked their anger and how their bodies responded physically and emotionally. By explaining how someone responds to anger, it starts the process of taking ownership for their actions. When making decisions on how they would respond differently in the future, they are building bridges to a healthier thought/reaction process.

Date:

Intensity Level 1-10   1 2 3 4 5 6 7 8 9 10 (circle one)

Explain the situation that sparked your anger?

What were you experiencing physically and emotionally?

How did you respond to your anger?

How would you respond differently if the same situation came up again?

Anger is necessary part of living. We all get angry, and anger in itself is not a negative emotion. How we respond to anger determines if our actions are working for or against us.

Depression is part of the grieving process. By recognizing the symptoms, people are more likely to reach out for help before getting stuck in the pit of despair.

Signs of depression

- Feelings of hopelessness
- Feelings of sadness or irritability
- Loss of interest in sex and activities once enjoyed
- Changes in weight or appetite
- Over- or under-eating
- Changes in sleeping patterns
- Over or under amounts of sleep
- Unrealistic feelings of guilt or shame
- Inability to concentrate or remember things
- Difficulty making decisions
- Fatigue and/or loss of energy
- Restlessness
- Complaints of physical aches and pains for which no medical causes can be found
- Thoughts of suicide or death

Everyone has ups and downs, combined with moments of sadness. When people experience several of the above symptoms for two or more weeks, it may be beneficial for them to seek help.

Survivors often have a limited vocabulary in terms of understanding and expressing their true feelings and emotions. This is common for all men. The closer we want to come to feeling whole, the more we want to be able to express all the feelings and emotions that accompany being human. The list below is a great tool to view when completing exercises pertaining to the identification and expression of feelings.

Feelings list

Angry feelings: angry, annoyed, bitter, frustrated, furious, hateful, mad, peeved, rage

Worry feelings: bothered, uneasy, unsettled, restless

Wanting feelings: empty, gypped, jealous, lonely, longing, lustful, rejected

Confidence feelings: bold, confident, eager, energetic, helpful, inspired, keen, powerful, sure, strong, trusting

Satisfied feelings: adequate, blissful, calm, glad, grateful, peaceful, satisfied

Pain feelings: agony, grief, guilt, hurt, remorse, shame

Disoriented feelings: ambivalent, confused, disoriented, flustered, sceptical, suspicious, zany

<u>Sad feelings</u>: low, melancholy, miserable, sad, sorrowful, weepy

<u>Fear feelings</u>: anxious, fear, frightened, hysterical, nervous, petrified, scared, terrified, threatened, vulnerable

<u>Pleasurable feelings</u>: affection, blissful, cheerful, delighted, elated, high, joy, pleased, loving, sexy

<u>Unmotivated feelings</u>: apathy, exhausted, hopeless, helpless, lazy, lethargic, powerless

Another great awareness tool is the emotion/reaction/ assessment. This exercise has proven to be an eye-opener for survivors. It is another exercise to illustrate how people respond to their feelings. By becoming aware of how these responses, they can choose healthier options.

Emotion/reaction/assessment exercise

Pick a situation in your life that was emotionally overloading:

Part #1 <u>EMOTION</u>

List your feelings and emotions connected to this event.

Part #2 <u>REACTIONS</u>

List how you responded (coping skills) to these feelings and emotions.

Part #3 <u>ASSESSMENT</u>

Which coping skills were healthy and which were unhealthy?

Part #4 <u>MOVING ON</u>

What new coping skills would you like to try in the future?

The house of self-respect

Members often talk about feeling out of balance; how they couldn't find a routine that helped them feel good about themselves and how their lives felt unmanageable and hectic. One man from a previous group spoke positively about his life and his recovery. There seemed to be an inner peace about him. He was content with himself, and he was a far different person than several years prior. This person described how he had maintained his health by updating and monitoring his "house of self-respect." He kept a copy of this house taped to the wall in his bedroom. Whenever his life felt out of balance, he would review the illustration of this house and make the appropriate changes in his life. This man was able to balance his lifestyle with the aid of an illustration.

The "House of Self-respect" is an exercise often completed in both individual counselling and group. This helps people evaluate their present lifestyle and think of ways to enhance their quality of life. They envisioned themselves as a developer, designing a "blueprint" for their own self-respect. By planning for their futures, they were automatically moving towards "moving on." To build this house, they took a blank piece of paper and drew a large square box representing the framework for their house. They divided this square into different size rectangles. The design can be very simple or more elaborate; however, most people design a basic frame.

The group chose to build their individual homes on large flip chart paper. This box represented the exterior walls of their house. Next, they decided what rooms they would like to put in their house. Each room represented a portion of their life that was important to them, such as: time alone, family, friends, education, etc. Like any house, some rooms were larger than others. The rooms they wished to spend the most amount of time in were the largest. When they built these rooms, they remembered to acknowledge their needs and lifestyle. It included all the aspects of their life that they needed to feel good about themselves.

In a regular home, someone would spend time in each room. Each room in the house needed to be visited from time to time or it would decay and wither. Every once in a while, people have to renovate or put a fresh coat of paint on the walls. This was no different in their "house of self-respect." They expected to spend time in each room they constructed. This included time with: their children, their partners, their friends, their sisters, their brothers, or anything else that was important or necessary to them. It can contain rooms for volunteering, hobbies, being a husband, being a father, or going on a vacation. Each room represents something that is important.

Most members thought they had rooms in their present homes that were creating problems for them. They looked at those rooms and decided to make adjustments so they would feel good in that part of their house. If adjustment were impossible, they renovated and built a new room.

Since these rooms are based on their needs, it was important they tended to them in proportion to the size of the room. If they felt unbalanced in their life, they looked at their design and asked themselves if they were spending enough time in each area of the house. This helped them balance and integrate the different areas of their life into their scheduling of time.

One man's "house of self-respect"

One person chose to draw both his "old house," that represented his lifestyle within the last year, and his "new house," that represented his future goals.

His old house

This old house was an illustration of his lifestyle prior to group. He drew a house that was plain, dark, and gloomy. There were no doors or windows in that house, no yard to sit in, and he was confined to the inside. His goal was to create a more balanced lifestyle for himself and put more joy into his life.

His new house

He drew a lovely picture a new home that included windows and doors. These doors had a significant value to him. He talked about one door representing freedom, giving him a choice to leave or stay. Another door opened up into a big yard with a beautiful shade tree. The sun was shining and the birds were singing. This man pictured himself sitting under this tree relaxing and enjoying his surroundings. He was proud of his new home and looked forward to redirecting how he used his energy. When life seemed out of balance, he would look at his drawing and determine if he was spending enough time in each room.

After each member completed their drawings, they presented their home to the group. One man was not happy with his new house and constructed a new drawing at home and presented to the group the following week.

The group process is truly a great experience. There is something magical about a group of people sharing freely of themselves. Anytime you can be in a room with people who are being "real" with each other, the outcome is often a beautiful human experience. It seems fitting to end this book with the top fifteen quotes from group.

Top fifteen quotes from group

- "Never confuse the abnormality of the abuse with the abnormality of yourself. What happened to you was wrong and abnormal, and you are responding perfectly normally to an abnormal situation."
- "Anger is like gasoline. If you use it wisely, it will drive you to where you want to go. If you use it unwisely, it will blow up in your face."
- "You are responsible for your feelings and emotions and others are responsible for theirs."
- "It is easy for any of us to get angry. But to be angry with the correct person — to the correct level — at the correct moment — for the correct reason — and using the correct method to resolve the problem — that is not easy."
- "You cannot make a flower grow by pulling on it."
- "Less is more."
- "Good mental health is not the absence of stress. Dealing with stress as it occurs creates good mental health."
- "You cannot change others, you can only change yourself."
- "The small changes you make now turn into huge differences later."
- "People are human beings not human doings." (Warren Farrell)
- "Time alone does not heal, but dealing effectively with time, does."

- "If you want to be happy, never judge, blame, criticize, or compare. This holds true when relating to yourself and others."
- "Be careful how you talk to your children, for your children will turn into adults and talk to themselves in the same fashion."
- "Grieving is not a choice, but healing from grief is."
- "Wherever you are in your recovery is exactly where you should be."

Some of these quotes came from group members, and some are from unknown authors.

Thank you for accompanying these brave men on their journey. Hopefully, their sharing will help you with your journey.

Annotated Bibliography

Alberti, R. (1990). Your Perfect Right. Sixth revised edition. Impact Publishers. This guide to assertive living is well written in a concise and readable format that promotes gender equality in human relationships. It helps the reader build confidence in standing up for themselves and finding their true voice.

Bass, E., and Davis L. (1988). The Courage to Heal. Harper and Row Publishing. Although this guide is written predominately for women, many men will find this easy to read format helpful in their recovery process. I particularly like the thirteen stages of recovery outlined throughout the text. The material in this book is good, but could be even better and reach out to a larger audience if it included a chapter on men's issues.

Burns, D. (1980). Feeling Good. Avon Books. This book gives a drug-free method on how to deal with depression. Dr. Burns uses a cognitive therapy approach to healing. I agree with the author's point of view that our feelings are a mirrored image of our thoughts, but I think he is missing a big component by not recognizing that our thoughts can also be a mirrored image of our feelings. The feeling part of healing is essential. This book does a good job of describing the various cognitive distortion people experience.

Copeland, M. (1992). The Depression Workbook. New Harbinger Publications, Inc. This guide is designed for people living with depression and manic depression. I focused mostly on the information pertaining to bipolar depression. The material is well written and easy to read, with many practical exercises. What I like most about this book is the recognition of alternative methods in recovery.

Crowder, A. (1993). <u>Opening the Door</u>. Family and Children's Services of the Waterloo Region. This text has a variety of offerings from clinical psychologists that focuses on various treatment modalities for men recovering from sexual abuse. I focused on those areas relating to the impact of cultural beliefs and stereotypes. I agree with the author that many survivors move through a four phase model from breaking silence, to a victim phase, to a survivor phase, and to a thriver stage.

Davis, L. (1990). <u>The Courage to Heal Workbook.</u> Harper and Row, Publishing, Inc. This is an excellent self-help book that can be used individually or in counselling. There is a series of exercises that brings the reader through the various stages of recovery. My main focus was exploring how anger relates to male sexual abuse recovery.

Fisher, B. (1981). <u>Rebuilding.</u> Impact Publishers. This book is one of the best books written for people rebuilding their lives after a love relationship ends. Many men are jolted into disclosing the sexual abuse they were subjected to as children after a major loss like a divorce. This step-by-step guide can be a useful tool that touches on the many concerns a divorced survivor may confront in his recovery process.

French, M. (1965). <u>The Way of the Pilgrim.</u> Harper, San Francisco. This easy to read book describes the spiritual journey of one man and his travels through the mid-nineteenth century through Russia and Siberia while visiting monasteries. His constant search for the meaning of "praying without ceasing" illustrates the faith of this pilgrim. Although I learned a lot from this brave eastern man, I find it difficult to believe that the average present day westerners could practice his teachings within the culture we live in.

Haldane, S. (1984). Emotional First Aid. Irvington Publishers, Inc., New York. This hard to find book is well recommended by professionals working with male survivors of sexual abuse recovery. The main focus is to communicate the basic knowledge of ways to relieve emotional stress. The author expresses how each person's experience is unique, but the basic emotions and biological aspects are universal. He speaks in detail about the body's physical response to grief, anger, fear, and joy.

Lenfest, D. (1991). Men Speak Out. Health Communications, Inc. This text is written using an interview format. The author David Lenfest interviews John Lee, Ken Richardson, Robert J. Ackerman, Terry Kellog, Mike Lew and Pat Mellody. These six men are well known in the field of men's issues. The main focus is conscious living and the direction of the men's movement. A common theme presented throughout this book is co-dependency.

Lee J. (1993). Facing the Fire. Bantam Books. This book focuses on releasing anger in a healthy fashion. It talks about why men need to release anger using safe and healthy methods. Practical exercises are available for those wishing to explore their anger further.

Lew, M. (1988). Victims no Longer. Nevraumont Pub. Co., New York. This is an excellent book describing the effects of male childhood sexual abuse. I focused on the areas pertaining to men in support groups. This book is well written and covers a wide range of male sexual abuse recovery issues.

Mathews, F. (1995). Combining Voices. National Clearinghouse on Family Violence. The author of this text addresses both male and female sexual abuse recovery issues. What I like most is his views on recovery from the perspective of the male experience. He recognizes that men and women have different challenges that need to be addressed in their healing journeys. I agree with his view that men and women need to work together if we hope to eradicate the many concerns regarding sexual abuse.

Mathews, F. (1996). The Invisible Boy. National Clearinghouse on Family Violence. This text focuses on the victimization of male children and teens. The author looks at interpersonal violence from a male perspective. Dr. Fred Mathews (1996) challenges many of the statistics presently used in a woman-centred approach to sexual abuse healing.

Meth, R., Pasick R., Gordon, B., Allen, J., Feldman, L. (1990). Men in Therapy. Guildford Press. This excellent book can help men create a positive framework towards healthy masculinity. The author supports the view that masculinity is socially constricted and not a true representation of objective reality.

Sonkin, D. and Durphy, M. (1989). Learning to Live Without Violence. Volcano Press, Inc. This book is written in a workbook style with questions at the end of each chapter. It is written for both men who are violent, and men who have fears of becoming violent. I agree with the three choices men have when confronted with anger. He states you can either stuff it, escalate it, or direct it. A useful portion of this book is the explanation of anger journals.

Staudacher, C. (1994). Men in Grief. New Harbinger Publications, Inc. This book focuses on men grieving the death of a loved one, but is also useful material for men experiencing any loss. I agree with the authors view on meeting grief head on, by travelling through the core or centre, and experiencing and expressing the feelings and emotions connected to this loss. The writer helps to fill a void in grief literature for men.

Walter, J., and Peller, J. (1992). Becoming Solution-Focussed in Brief Therapy. Brunner/Mazel. This well written book illustrates a positive approach to short-term therapy. It focuses on moving a client towards a solution orientated future without the need to go back in time and address issues from the past. The writer describes this therapy as moving away from a problem orientated type of counselling. Although there are many good visualization exercises throughout this text, I wonder if the results of this type of therapy are short-term. I believe the work may address symptoms but not problems. Unless you address problems, the client will always need symptoms.

Weber, D. (1991). Angry? Do you Mind if I Scream? Health Communications, Inc. This worthwhile handbook demonstrates how anger is the missing link to healthy recovery. It is full of practical exercises that help some people gain awareness in creating their own personal anger action plan. This book is very easy reading and yet very factual.

Whitfield, C. (1989). Healing the Child Within. Health Communications Incorporated. Although this book focuses on adult children of alcoholics, it can be used as a resourceful guide for the recovery of childhood sexual abuse. The author provides the reader with an excellent one page pictorial graph that summarizes the stages of recovery (Whitfield, 1989 pg.120). This text addresses the importance of healing the inner child.

Whiting, G. (video, 2001) When Girls Do It. An unflinching look at the motivations of female sexual predators and the devastating effects on their victims. This documentary reveals the human reality behind sexual abuse by women; healing those who have survived abuse, treating female offenders and preventing countless other children from becoming victims. Featuring powerful interviews and compelling testimony, it shows how important it is to acknowledge the enormity of female sexual offences, and encourages victims to speak out against this devastating crime.

Books referenced:

Alberti, R. (1990). Your Perfect Right. Sixth revised edition. Impact Publishers.

Aristotle (1926). The Nicomachean Ethics. Harvard University Press.

Bass, E., and Davis L. (1988). The Courage to Heal. Harper and Row Publishers.

Bootzin, R. and Acocella, J. (1998). Abnormal Psychology. Fifth Edition. Random House Inc.

Briere, J. (1989). Therapy for Adults Molested as Children. Springer Publishing Company.

Burns, D. (1980). Feeling Good. Avon Books.

Burns, D. (1989). The Feeling Good Handbook. Penguin Books.

Copeland, M. (1992). The Depression Workbook. New Harbinger Publications, Inc.

Crowder, A. (1993). Opening the Door. Family and children's services of the Waterloo region.

Davis, L. (1990). The Courage to Heal Workbook. Harper and Row Publishing, Inc.

Fisher, B. (1981). Rebuilding. Impact Publishers.

French, M. (1965). The Way of the Pilgrim. Harper San Francisco.

Fujishin, R. (1997). Discovering the Leader Within. Acada Books, Inc.

Haldane, S. (1984). Emotional First Aid. Irvington Publishers, Inc., New York.

Janov, A. (1970). The Primal Scream. New York.

Jukubowski, P. and Lange, A. (1978). The Assertive Option. Research Press.

Keen, S. (1991). Fire in the Belly. New York, MacMillan Publishing Co.

Kopp, S. (1972). If You See Buddha on the Street, Kill Him. Science and Behaviour Books.

Lee, J. (1993). Facing the Fire. Bantam Books.

Lee, J. (1987). The Flying Boy. Health Communication, Inc.

Lenfest, D. (1991). Men Speak Out. Health Communications, Inc.

Lew, M. (1999). Leaping Upon the Mountains. North Atlantic Books. Berkley, California.

Lew, M. (1998). Victims No Longer. Harper and Row, Publishers, New York.

Mathews, F. (1995). Combining Voices. National Clearinghouse on Family Violence.

Mathews, F. (1996). The Invisible Boy. National Clearinghouse on Family Violence.

Meth, R., Pasick R., Gordon, B., Allen, J., Feldman, L. (1990). Men in Therapy. Guilford Press.

Peck, S. (1978). The Road Less Travelled. Simon and Schuster.

Rogers, C. (1961). On Becoming a Person. Houghton Mifflin Company. Boston.

Rogers, C. (1965). Client-Centered Therapy. Houghton Mifflin Company. Boston.

Rosen, R. (1975). Psychobabble. McClelland and Stewart Ltd.

Rosenberg, K. (1994). Talk to Me. G.P. Putnam's Sons New York.

Rubin, T. (1969). The Angry Book. Collier Books.

Seligman, M. (1994). What You Can Change and What You Can't. Alfred A. Knopf, Inc.

Sonkin, D. and Durphy, M. (1989). Learning to Live Without Violence. Volcano Press, Inc.

Staudacher, C. (1994). Men in Grief. New Harbinger Publications, Inc.

Walter, J., and Peller, J. (1992). Becoming Solution-Focussed in Brief Therapy. Brunner/Mazel.

Weber, D. (1991). Angry? Do You Mind If I Scream? Health Communications, Inc.

Whitfield, C. (1989). Healing the Child Within. Health Communications Incorporated.

Lectures referenced:

Bichekas, G. (1992). Adults Molested as Children. Sarnia-Lambton Sexual Abuse Treatment Network.

Cortese, L. (1998). Understanding and Coping with Psychosis. Canadian Mental Health Association.

Guldner, C. (1997). Eyes Movement Desensitization and Reprocessing (Introductory). University of Guelph, Family Studies.

Guldner, C. (1997). Eyes Movement Desensitization and Reprocessing (Advanced). University of Guelph, Family Studies.

Guldner, C. (1997). Man's Search for Connection. 19th Annual Guelph conference and training institute on sexuality.

Guldner, C. (1994). Solution Orientated Therapy. 16th Annual Guelph Conference and Training Institute on Sexuality.

Guldner, C. (1997). Solution Orientated Therapy. 19th Annual Guelph Conference and Training Institute on Sexuality.

Hawkins, R., Crowder, A. (1997). Therapeutic Pathways to Health for Male Survivors of Sexual Abuse. 19th Annual Guelph conference and training institute on sexuality.

Hunter, R., and Little, D. (1993). Critical Education Therapy. Harbourd Centre for Critical Education/Therapy.

Hunter, R., and Little, D. (1994). Critical Education Therapy. Harbourd Centre for Critical Education/Therapy.

Kushiner, L. (1992). Working with Male Sexual Abuse Survivors. 1st London and regional conference.

McMorrow, K. (1994). Techniques for Helping Clients/ Students Deal with Their Anger. 16th Annual conference and training institute on sexuality.

Middleton-Moz, J. (1994). Affirming the Positive Power of the Human Spirit.

Petrimioulx, L. (1995). Adolescence, Post-Traumatic and Dissociative Disorders. 17th Annual Guelph conference and training institute on sexuality.

Saunders, J. (1995). Grieving. Chatham Mental Health Kent.

Shulman, L. (1994). Group Dynamics. Wallaceburg conference.

Thesis, J., Naus P. (1997). Fatherly Affirmation. 19th Annual Guelph Conference and Training Institute on Sexuality.

About the Author

Tom Wilken is the owner of Hope and Healing Associates, program co-ordinator for the Silence to Hope Project, and lives in the village of Erieau, Ontario. He was the only counsellor in Canada to have worked for a Sexual Assault Crisis Centre that had a separate satellite office for a men's program. Tom also wrote the *Adult Survivors of Child Sexual Abuse Overview Paper* for Health Canada. He has been working with The Ministry of Children and Youth Services and the Ministry of Community Safety and Correction Services as a probation officer for the last six years. Tom has a Bachelor of Arts degree in psychology and counselling from Goddard College, Vermont, and a business marketing diploma from St. Clair College, Windsor, Ontario.